Not All Bad Comes to Harm You

Not All Bad Comes to Harm You

OBSERVATIONS OF A CANCER SURVIVOR

JANICE MOCK

NOT ALL BAD COMES TO HARM YOU
OBSERVATIONS OF A CANCER SURVIVOR

iUniverse books may be ordered through booksellers or by contacting:

iUniverse
1663 Liberty Drive
Bloomington, IN 47403
www.iuniverse.com
1-800-Authors (1-800-288-4677)

Because of the dynamic nature of the Internet, any web addresses or links contained in this book may have changed since publication and may no longer be valid. The views expressed in this work are solely those of the author and do not necessarily reflect the views of the publisher, and the publisher hereby disclaims any responsibility for them.

Any people depicted in stock imagery provided by Thinkstock are models, and such images are being used for illustrative purposes only.
Certain stock imagery © Thinkstock.

ISBN: 978-1-4917-6708-5 (sc)
ISBN: 978-1-4917-6709-2 (e)

Library of Congress Control Number: 2015908551

Print information available on the last page.

iUniverse rev. date: 7/27/2015

To Dr. Stephen Hufford, who saved my life.

And to my wife, Carole, who chose to share hers with me.

Be happy for this moment.
This moment is your life.
—Omar Khayyam

Contents

Acknowledgments

I thank my friend and writer extraordinaire Kirsten Mickelwait for her support and hard work in helping me edit the various drafts of this missive, and my wife, Carole, and my dear friends Ernie, Joanie, and Patrick for lumbering through those first attempts at getting words on paper. I also thank musical artist Jane Siberry, for allowing me to reprint portions of her work, and Christopher Gage, Laura Haber, Alan Scofield, and Kelly Snow for allowing me to use their beautiful photographs and artwork.

My gratitude also extends to my dear friends and family who stood by me with help, comfort, and care when I so desperately needed it during my cancer treatment. But for you, this story couldn't be told. You all know who you are, from coast to coast, and I thank you from the bottom of my heart for your generosity of spirit and endless kindness.

Prologue

"BUT I'VE GOT NOTHING TO SAY."

That was my first response. My girlfriend and I were sitting at a hideaway table in the back patio of a Murano trattoria when she suggested that I write a book about my experience fighting cancer and the resultant change in my life. But what could I possibly say that others hadn't said a hundred (or a thousand) times before? Sadly, in this day and age, fighting cancer has become as commonplace as fighting the flu. Hundreds of books have been written about personal struggles and survival, either by the cancer victims themselves or the loved ones left behind after cancer won. What could I possibly add?

Actually, I was at first defensive, then practically indignant. I don't know why her suggestion struck me in such an unwelcome way. Perhaps it was the thought of more responsibility, adding just one more thing to my to-do list. And though writing a book is an unquestionably daunting task, there may have been more to it than that.

Today I look back on my initial reaction as a reluctance to readdress the experiences I had already lived through once and look at them in the cold, hard light of day. Maybe I didn't want to feel responsible for what I might say to others, or what they might hear, about those experiences. This is about people's lives, after all. You can't just willy-nilly jot a few notes on a page without taking responsibility for them. Words have power.

The other factor—this notion of everyone having said everything there is to say about cancer—I only understood just recently. It boils down to this: to tell someone that I have nothing to say about this whole mess would be like telling a photographer not to take a picture of the sunset. I mean, it's been done, hasn't it? Over and over. How many more sunset pictures do we need, really?

But maybe that's the point. Every photographer sees the sunset in a different way. Same sunset, different viewpoint. Some photographs we love; others not so much. Some inspire us; others do not. Sharing my story is really no more than sharing a perspective that is singularly mine and no one else's. Yep, thousands of people have cancer. Thousands of people are fighting it. Thousands more are living with it. I am just one of those thousands, but I share my story with you with the hope that at least one of you will find some new insight, strength, or self-awareness in my words.

So, here goes.

Flying Coach

SEPTEMBER 2012

I HAVE CANCER.

Okay. There. I said it.

When I was going through chemotherapy they told me I might experience periods of cold, numbness in my limbs, headaches, and cramps. What they didn't tell me is that a long-haul airplane flight could cause the same thing.

This tale began in row 22J on a flight from Rome to San Francisco— in coach. Need I say more?

I detest flying coach, having enjoyed several years of "platinum" status amenities while traveling for work. First class is not something I can generally afford, but it was a perk for being forced to spend so much time away from home. Once you've languished in the luxurious leather seats, enjoyed actual legroom and free-flowing wine, and savored a few tasty meals, flying coach is almost unbearable. Even today I still buy everything with a credit card that lets me accrue miles for upgrades, which is about as glamorous as first-class traveling gets these days.

Yet there I found myself, in economy class, when my upgrade didn't come through.

"I'm sorry, this last seat is for VIP-status upgrades only," the

1

unhelpful man at the counter had said. In other words: you're screwed, lady; please enjoy your ten-hour flight back to the States.

"God help me," I moaned under my breath.

There's only so much you can do in ten hours while crammed like a sardine in the back of the plane. We've all been there, so I know you can relate. The guy in front of you tilts his seat all the way back the minute the wheels leave the ground, and for the next eternity you sit with your knees crammed into your tray table while your butt goes numb. You try to accomplish the impossible task of sleeping bolt upright, all the while freezing from the air-conditioning. Then you are nudged by the very kind flight attendant (who just wants off the plane as much as you do) as he hands out little snack crackers and dreams of Maui in the summertime. The entire adventure in the little silver tube is a study in socioeconomics and social moorings.

I took the crackers, then leaned over to my girlfriend and said, "I wonder what they're having in first class, don't you?"

She suggested I go and ask, no doubt because I was worse than a two-year-old, squirming around in my tiny seat, sick to death of looking at the bald spot on the head of the guy in front of me, shining away.

"I wonder if they're napping in their comfy first-class beds right now," I said. Yep, beds on a plane. They're reserved for the platinum members because people in the real world can't afford to pay US dollars for one of those seats—not unless they are multimillionaires or rock stars or both.

Just as the tingling sensation in my feet began to overtake the rest of my body, I started musing on how we all came together at forty-two thousand feet somewhere over the Atlantic. Each person had his or her own story.

Was that sweet-looking couple on vacation? How about that guy traveling alone; was he a terrorist? The little girl across the aisle seemed so nice, sharing her candy with her brother—the product of a good upbringing, no doubt. And who were the four older women traveling together, circling round and round the aisles of the airplane to fend off thrombosis? Why was getting old such a pain?

Me? I was a cancer survivor. Sitting on that plane marked almost one year to the day since my last chemotherapy treatment, which—despite my bellyaching—made flying coach seem like a luxury cruise. How many of my fellow passengers were also cancer survivors, I wondered? Half? A third? Practically everyone has some kind of cancer these days, or knows someone who does. Wouldn't it be awful to have survived cancer only to die at the hands of the would-be terrorist hijacker in Row 23? What would have been the point of that mammoth effort? I would be so pissed.

I decided to amuse myself with my iPad and start jotting down a few thoughts about this whole cancer thing, but the societal laboratory in the sky distracted me. It's the haves versus the have-nots. It's the crying children, the couples sleeping on each other's shoulders, and the old people who can't sit for very long. It's everyone just trying to get along in a small, cramped, completely unrealistic space where each must respect the confines of his or her little econo-seat/cell and try (mostly) to ignore his or her fellow passengers and pretend they aren't there. But at forty-two thousand feet, we were bound together loosely with a genuine desire to get that plane back on the ground safely and—after 9/11—to tackle and beat the hell out of anyone who might interfere with our collective goal. We are bound together by our survival instincts.

Maybe that's what makes people fight cancer head on in the first place—our survival instincts. But more on that later.

Meanwhile, six hours into the flight, with four to go, surely there were others back here with me who also were losing touch with their nether regions. What kept them in their seats and behaving appropriately? What if I stood up then and there and asked to see a show of hands of those who hated American Airlines for reneging on their "more room in coach" promise and reinserting the extra two rows in the back to generate more revenue? How much money could the airline lose if it took a foot or two out of first class and provided a more humane traveling experience to those holding down the rear? Perhaps, just perhaps, they could have found something softer for us to sit on than an upside-down flotation device? Were the first-class passengers sitting on flotation devices? How much money were we talking about anyway? Was it the difference between operating an airline or not? Or was it about profit margins, no matter how small?

Ah yes, profit.

I cannot tell you how many times that word came up in my mind and in my conversations during the past year.

Now, in cancer-survivor world, I'm fatigued by the constant commentary on profit. Financial gain. M-O-N-E-Y. People who have none need it, and those who have it and don't need it just want more. Corporate greed is rampant. It's all about money, all the time. It is the singular Holy Grail.

Well, in many ways, it *is* about the money. At least that's what I assume my mortgage holder believes: no payment equals no roof over my head. The grocery store also seems to favor money in exchange for milk and eggs.

This leads most of us to live a daily existence sometimes referred to as the grind. We get up early, go to work, come home, feed the kids and the dog (not necessarily in that order), pay a few bills, and go to bed late. Sleep. Repeat. Five days in a row; sometimes more. We do this to keep the roof and the eggs and the milk. The weekends come and go far too quickly; then we're at it again. The time spent reading a book, listening to music, or visiting friends is reduced to those few hours or minutes that can be squeezed in-between.

What's crazy to me is how the enjoyment of life takes a seat in coach, while work, work, work always rides first class. How can we change the seating arrangement? And why must we spend so much of our lives working, only to retire at sixty-five (or later—one of my law firm partners is still working at age ninety!) and hope we have enough time to enjoy what is left of our lives. This is a collective complaint many of us have had for a long time.

There's something about having cancer, though, that brings the workday world into stark relief against the backdrop of real living. A heightened awareness becomes part of your everyday existence. Each week, each day, each moment matters. And it matters a lot.

The old cliché goes something like this: we're all going to die someday. Yes, it's true. No one is getting out of here alive. But that amorphous concept fades quickly when someone hands you a cancer diagnosis on a silver platter. Suddenly, your time is up. You then know for *sure* you're going to die, and *how* you're going to die. Kapow! Believe me, this isn't child's play. All that crap about live for today, smell the roses, and the rest jumps off the page and smacks you in the head. Suddenly, billing another hour at the law firm doesn't matter, and it doesn't matter in a big, big way.

I sat there reflecting on the people I had met in Italy, and the wonderful experiences we had shared. True or false, it seemed to me that Italians are just happier. Their culture seems more satisfying. Working less, they still manage to keep roofs over their heads, all the while enjoying monthlong (or longer) vacations. How do they do it?

Emulating the Tuscan lifestyle is all but impossible in the States because societal norms just don't support such a thing. Here, it's all about working like a dog to make ends meet; it's not about lingering over a plate of cheeses and vibrant, hand-gesturing conversations with friends. Or two-hour siestas. It's not about a long, relaxing dinner where the check doesn't arrive until you ask for it. They're not about turning tables in Italy to make another buck. It's about enjoying each moment. "La dolce far niente." "The sweetness of doing nothing." *That's* what they're about.

Sitting on that plane, I wondered whether I would ever see Italy again, or enjoy another glass of Brunello, or ride up to Radicofani on my bike. But one thing I knew for sure was that I would take home what I had learned about bountiful living and apply it to my own, very changed life. I had survived cancer, but now I was learning to *live*.

First Understandings

MARCH 2011

I was driving home from the San Jose courthouse one day with the top down on the car. I love my midlife-crisis convertible. It was an outlandish treat for myself when I turned fifty (maybe prompted in part by the valet guy at my office building who kept calling my sedan an "old lady" car). The California sun was shining, and the drive north along the famous San Andreas fault line was just glorious. The beauty of the journey felt disconnected from the fact that I had just been diagnosed with cancer, although the doctors didn't yet know what kind. A positron emission tomography scan (PET scan sounds deceivingly friendlier) in a few days would reveal the unknown.

I was hovering in that imaginary world in which you decide that someone has simply made a mistake at the lab. Denial has an ingenious way of preventing a psychotic breakdown as your mind adjusts to new information. Yet despite the devastating news I'd received only days earlier, I was experiencing an overwhelming sense of peace. It seemed odd, under the circumstances. I felt the sun, breathed the air, and took in the coastal mountain range with more than a fleeting glance. I said to myself, out loud, "If this is the end of my life, I am happy to have experienced it." My appreciation and understanding of my good fortune was deep. It was some kind of magical break in the unfolding drama to be able to experience existence in a way that I never had before.

I've always loved the Carl Sagan film *Contact*. In it, Jodie Foster delivers one of the more memorable lines in cinema. She is asked whether, as a scientist, she believes there is life on other planets.

"Well," she says, "the universe is a pretty big place. It's bigger than anything anyone has ever dreamed of before. So if it's just us, it seems like an awful waste of space."

I now know why I liked that movie. I felt, indeed I knew, that there was something more elsewhere. And in that same moment I understood that my experience on this planet was limited to a flash in time—our years or decades are merely brief episodes in an immeasurable existence. My visit to this planet has been a treat: the oceans, the redwoods, the sky, snow in the mountains, the Grand Canyon, Yosemite. These wonderful, beautiful things are here for us to experience during our visit to Earth. Suddenly, I was overwhelmed with gratitude for having been able to enjoy them.

At the same time I also knew that more lay elsewhere and beyond. Now, I'm not into organized religion of any kind or variety, so it wasn't that. It was something else entirely that I had yet to put my finger on.

Lost and Found

MARCH 2011

Okay, so I'm a little bit of an Italophile. It's not like my whole house is filled with hand-painted ceramics or anything, but I do love the beauty of Italy, the food, the melodic language, and the people. I'm especially fond of Tuscan Brunello wine from the beautiful Montalcino region. Several years ago a good friend introduced me to Italy, and after a whirlwind tour of Rome—during which I had to see all the sights—we headed for Venice and then west to Portofino. I fell in love. Portofino is a jewel on the Italian Riviera. It reminds me of Sausalito, California, with its beautiful oceanic setting, only it is, well, older. And Italian. Whether strolling along the waterfront or climbing up to the Church of San Giorgio, I felt alive and present amid the vibrant flowers and spectacular geography and was ever-so-grateful to be there.

To my great delight, the following year I finally took my dream vacation—a bike tour through Tuscany. A group of friends was going, someone had dropped out, and the others invited me along. I was elated. We stayed at a beautiful villa and rode each day to surrounding *poggios* (Tuscan hillsides); then we were carted back to the house by our phenomenal tour guides, Marco and Giuliana, where we lounged by the pool, napped, then enjoyed cooking classes and a sumptuous dinner we made ourselves. Three generations of gracious Italian women lovingly shared their secrets of Tuscan cooking; we rolled pasta by hand. It was an amazing experience, and I could not wait to go back. To prepare for the trip, I had tried my hand at learning Italian from one of those little books that teach you *il ristorante* (restaurant), *albergo* (hotel), *vorrei un bicchiare di vino* (I would like a glass of wine), and the like. Though I was far from accomplished at the task, it was interesting and fun, and I enjoyed many impromptu conversations with the locals.

A couple of years later I decided it would be a good brain exercise—and perhaps staving off dementia?—to study the language further. Learning a new language after age fifty is a challenge, to say the least, but I was committed. One of my friends had suggested the idea, so we rounded up two others and went to class once a week. We spent eighteen weeks with a saucy, storytelling young woman named Laura, who entertained and guided us through the various conjugations of that difficult but romantic language.

Laura was a bit of a free spirit; she had moved to Rome years earlier on a whim with but a few dollars and without knowing the language at all. She ended up living there for a long time, falling in love, setting up a home, and reveling in life in that wildly hectic city. She had returned to the United States just months before we met. We enjoyed our weekly evenings together, and I dedicated myself to the task of reading assignments and doing homework. Frequently, a couple of the gals and I wrapped up our Wednesday evenings at a local *ristorante*, owned and operated by a Neapolitan guy who not only served great food but also was charming, kind, and willing to listen to our novice Italian efforts. It was a wonderful time, and I was just getting the hang of those miserable conjugations when the news came.

The last night of class was supposed to be a celebration, and we had planned to take Laura to our Neapolitan friend's restaurant for a graduation dinner. We were very excited and had planned to attend our final class, then go.

But just days earlier I had gotten the phone call: my needle biopsy had come back positive. I had cancer—either stomach or ovarian, definitely something glandular—but they weren't sure what. A PET scan soon followed, leaving me in an awful limbo where I wouldn't know what kind of cancer it was until the pathology report was released. I was determined, though, to carry on with my life. As planned, I went to the last Italian class, but I didn't say anything to my classmates. Despite my best efforts, however, my attempted mental gymnastics and compartmentalization just weren't enough.

I fancied myself as pretty good at such things; I'd gone through a breakup during my first-year finals in law school and still managed to wrest good grades from the jaws of failure. I have always been able to control my thinking and set aside emotional issues in favor of more-pressing tasks. Being more of a linear thinker than an emotional responder has served me well in my life as a lawyer. That said, during our last class, Laura made a comment that hit home: something about never knowing what can happen in one's life. And just like that, the compartments collapsed. I could no longer keep the rising tide at bay; my eyes welling with tears, I excused myself from the room. After several minutes, my best friend, Erika, sought me out to see what was wrong. She found me in another room looking out the window and trying desperately to stop the flood. I inhaled. I swallowed. I could not meet her eyes. I had nothing to say because, at that moment, I knew nothing. I knew that I had cancer, but no more. And of all the people in the world I dreaded facing with this news, Erika was at the top of the list.

My dearest, dearest friend and sister-of-choice, Erika had already survived the hell of losing her beloved husband and my brother-in-every-respect, Mike. A tall, strapping British fellow, he had an unmatched wit and a congenial personality and was loved by one and all. A police sergeant in a nearby town, Mike struck an imposing figure in his uniform. To me, he was a big, lovable teddy bear of a friend and trusted confidante. He had died just over a year earlier from multiple myeloma. Misdiagnosed early on, Mike struggled and fought through two bone-marrow transplants, the last of which his body rejected. His final years were unbearably painful for him and heartbreaking for the rest of us, especially Erika. She was his 24/7 caretaker, moving to Austin, Texas, at one point near the end so Mike could fulfill his dream of owning his own home. He died in her arms at the MD Anderson Cancer Center in Houston.

Erika stood there looking at me, but I could not bear to open her wounds of sadness and bring her nightmare to life all over again. Instead, I said I was under a lot of pressure at work, but things were fine. Then I sucked it up, shoved my emotional thunderstorm back inside, and off we went to dinner.

The evening was more than a little surreal. The restaurant is one of my favorite hangouts, and a couple of longtime friends and neighbors were there when we arrived. There were lots of smiles and hellos and introductions, and our group was celebratory and festive. Meanwhile, I engaged in Olympic-worthy mental gymnastics, struggling mightily to enjoy our little graduation party while keeping my unspoken terror in check. It was exhausting, and by the time I got home I felt sick to my stomach from the effort.

A week or so later—once the diagnosis had been made and I'd revealed all the details—Laura learned about my plight and sent me the most beautiful postcard. It was a photograph of an unknown street and buildings in Rome, near where she once lived; on the back she had written:

> TRASTEVERE, ROMA
>
> JAN, when you get through all this I would love to see a picture of you standing in the middle of this entrance. (my house is the orange building on th far right, above the stairs) If I have been taught one very special thing living here all these years it would be this: "Non tutto il male viene per nuocere" = Not all bad comes to harm you... Con tutto il cuore bella anima mia.
> Laura. Vc

> Jan, when you get through all this, I would love to see a
> picture of you standing in the middle of this entrance …
> If I have been taught one very special thing, living here
> all these years, it would be this: "Non tutto i'l male
> viene per nuocere"—not all bad comes to harm you.

I received many "get well" and "thinking of you" cards but was so touched by this one that it found a place on the mantel in my bedroom. Nestled among my many talismans and lucky charms for improved health, the card represented a goal: I would get through my cancer treatment and one day return to Italy, find Laura's apartment, take a picture of myself standing in front of it, and send it to her.

The Diagnosis

FEBRUARY 2011

IT WAS ALMOST IMPERCEPTIBLE, THAT LITTLE LUMP IN MY NECK JUST above my left clavicle. I felt it one morning after waking up with my hand curled under my chin. *Huh*, I thought, then immediately checked the other side of my neck—nothing there. At first I figured I had strained a muscle. I'd been training pretty hard for the upcoming seven-day California AIDS Ride. I was in dance class twice a week, bicycling, and lifting weights. I felt great. But even so, here was this thing in my neck.

I puzzled over this thumb-sized lump for a few days, then one day in dance class, I asked my friend Joanie to check it out.

"What do you think this is?" I asked. "Could it be my thyroid?"

"Well, for starters, your thyroid is here, not there," she replied, gesturing toward the hollow at the base of her neck. Obviously, it was a good thing I had not gone to medical school. Feeling silly, I let her press here and there, after which she finally declared, "You should have it checked out. It's probably just a swollen lymph node or something."

Ah, the joys of getting older, I thought. *Random lumps appearing here and there. Nice.*

I made an appointment for the following week—no rush, you see; it was probably nothing—with my primary care physician, whom I'd seen exactly once in the last decade. I never spent much time (read: *any* time) at the doctor's office because I'd been blessed with terrific health.

I missed a call from the doctor's office canceling my appointment, and barely caught her as she was rushing out to get a broken tooth fixed. If I'd been a few minutes later, I would have missed her entirely.

Urging the front-desk assistant to let me see her, I said, "It will only take thirty seconds." *Just take a look at it, lady. No big deal.*

I was ushered quickly into an exam room where, exasperated because her staff didn't shoo me away, the doctor pressed once or twice on my neck and said it was probably just a swollen lymph node fighting off a cold. *I could have paid Joanie for this diagnosis.* Well, at least it was no big deal.

"Call me in a week if it's still there," she said matter-of-factly. Then she added, quite casually, "And for goodness sake, don't go searching on the Internet; that'll just keep you up at night. See you!" And with that, she walked, almost ran, through the door.

Back to the elevators I went with my swollen lymph node. *Guess Joanie could have been a doctor as well as a dancer; probably would have paid better. I must be catching a cold. But how weird that I don't feel sick.* My thoughtful little analysis paraded through my mind as I drove to the office.

Later that night at home, I couldn't resist. Sitting in the semidarkness in front of my computer, I Googled "swollen lymph node in neck."

Let me just say, I don't recommend a lot of Internet research for the very reason the doctor said: it will keep you up at night. Most of the stuff is just downright scary, some of it is misinformation, and all of it is overwhelming. But right there on the website of a renowned medical facility was a list of cancer symptoms, including a swollen lymph node in the neck. The hair on the back of mine stood up.

Alert! Surely not. I tried to remain calm as I watched this little thumb-size lump every day as if it were under a microscope. I felt it repeatedly for a week, trying to determine if it were changing in size, trying to talk myself into believing it was shrinking. *It is getting smaller, right? I must have measured incorrectly yesterday.* The days passed—seven of them. I decided to watch it for a few more days before I saw the doctor again. I called and made an appointment for about a week later. Surely, it would be gone by then.

No such luck. Though it had not grown, neither had it shrunk, and I found myself back at the doctor's office listening to her tell me about setting up an appointment with a surgeon. A surgeon?

"Why?" I asked.

"Because it may need to come out," she replied matter-of-factly. "It shouldn't be swollen like this."

Since doctors are almost never available immediately, I made an appointment with the surgeon many days hence. When we finally arrived, the receptionist in the small office greeted me and my little lump and asked us to take a seat.

I don't remember much of what the surgeon said to me at the time, because everything happened so fast; it was all a blur. But he examined me and then sent me downstairs for a chest x-ray and across the street to the lab for a needle biopsy. Needles! To say that I loathe and despise needles would be an understatement. I have never reconciled the benefits of being poked with sharp objects, whether they are used for putting something in or taking something out. You might say it is a phobia (and I don't have too many of those, not counting snakes).

Before I left his office, the nice doctor gave me a rundown of the myriad things it could be, now too many to recount. The only one I remember was the possibility that it could be cancer.

Cancer.

As I said, I hate needles, just hate 'em. Even as a little girl who had to get weekly allergy shots, I was never placated by the lollipops. I rarely had blood tests for this very reason, and donating blood was out of the question. Yet there I sat, during the last hour of the workday, on a cushiony, vinyl table in some tiny room in the pathologist's lab, waiting for a very nice man to give me "just a small stick" in my neck. Funny enough, it didn't hurt the way I imagined it would: a pinch, then a little draw of fluid. That was it. Chipper and cheery, the technician gave me the same list of possibilities the surgeon had reported. But the C word never came out of his mouth.

I headed home. Trying to manage my emotions around this new development, I put the top down on the car and drove through the awe-inspiring eucalyptus trees in the Presidio, winding my way through the federally protected land to the base of the Golden Gate Bridge. I breathed in deeply, trying to stop my mind from racing. *What could it be? Was this serious? Surely not. It was just a swollen lymph node. I was fine. I felt fine.*

In fact, I felt terrific. I had been training for the bicycling event, now just a month away, and was in pretty good shape. (Looking back later, I realized that I never actually visualized myself doing the ride, or sleeping in a tent at the campsites, or any of the other things that I had done many times before during such events. It was as if my subconscious already knew that I wouldn't make the journey.)

I took a last-minute turn after crossing the bridge and headed up the Marin Headlands to enjoy the cascading view to San Francisco, then wound down the west side toward the Pacific. The road down is so magnificent that car commercials are filmed there. But commercials were far from my mind at that point as I tried to keep a level head and not jump to conclusions.

I think it was a Friday when I got the call, maybe a Thursday; I don't know. I do know I was sitting in my office at the end of a busy day when the phone rang.

"Jan, this is Dr. Smith. We've got the results. Your chest x-ray looks great. Nothing. But there *is* cancer in that lymph node."

I froze. Nothing happened. My brain felt like it had jumped a track.

"Are you sure?" I said, somewhat incredulously. *Tests are frequently wrong, right?*

"The pathologist is pretty sure. He can't identify the cells exactly, but it looks glandular. Either stomach or ovarian. He's not sure. You'll need a PET scan."

My heart started pounding as if it sensed danger was imminent. My palms began to sweat. Fear. I could taste the fear at that moment; it's no cliché. The rest of the conversation evaporated. I hung up.

I did the only thing I could think to do. I called my law firm partner and friend, Patrick, but got his voice mail. Desperate, I dialed his cell phone, guessing he might be on his way home since it was after office hours.

"This is Patrick."

"Hi," I said. "Where are you?"

"On my way home. What's up?"

I didn't know what to say, how to start, how to explain. I didn't even try.

The words "I have cancer" spilled out, and I began to cry. I blubbered out the few details I knew, and the tears kept falling after we ended the call. I put my head in my hands, shocked. *What was I going to do?*

Disoriented. Alone. I don't know how long I sat there engulfed in fear of the unknown before my friend and partner walked through my office door and put his arms around me. He had turned around and come back.

As I came to realize many months later, this cancer thing was a gift in many unexpected ways. One of the most precious gifts would be knowing *exactly* who were my true friends and who were not. Patrick was a true friend. He dragged me out of that office and to a local pub, where I had two double cosmopolitans. We talked about life and death, and laughed at the challenges we sometimes face. My friend, and the martinis, buoyed me back to the surface as I recast the life I had once known into a new one that would take its place.

Sharing

MARCH 2011

IT TAKES AWHILE AT FIRST TO GRAPPLE WITH THE MEANING OF THE "cancer" news. It's a helluva scary topic, and until now, my conversations about it usually were pretty abstract. I'd raised money for cancer survivors and research; I'd had relatives who had died of cancer, but I never imagined for a moment it would be me. Or my life.

Although the martinis helped dampen the initial shock, it roared back when I had to confront my girlfriend, Andrea, with the news. When she arrived that night for dinner, she could tell immediately that something was wrong.

"I don't know how to tell you this," I started. The tears came then, welling up in my eyes and setting off alarms for her.

"What?" she begged. "What in the world is wrong?"

All I could say was this, "What would be the worst possible thing I could tell you?" My voice trailed off. I looked down, then up again and met her now-tearful eyes.

"I have cancer."

Looking back, I just don't know what is worse—getting the news yourself or having to tell someone who cares about you. It's all unfair, no matter what, but there is something so helpless about those who have to know the truth. Unlike you, there is nothing they can do. They can only be supportive, but they cannot don the armor and get on with the battle. They cannot take the cancer away. No one can.

It was then that I also realized how alone I truly was. It's not that Andrea didn't care about me, or that I didn't have wonderful friends to turn to. It was not that. It was my aloneness with my body and my diagnosis and my psyche and my emotions and everything else that was and is me. Doctors can diagnose and prescribe drugs, friends can bring groceries and send flowers, but no one but you can truly engage the enemy combatant.

There is nothing about that night that I will ever forget. Although I tried to keep up a brave front while telling Andrea the horrible news, all bravery melted away in the dark of night, and I found myself wide awake in the wee hours, contemplating the awfulness of what was to come. Tripping downstairs in the dark, I flung myself on the couch and sobbed uncontrollably into the pillows. My soon-to-be reality of chemotherapy needles, IVs, and poisoning my own body to try and beat the disease washed over me. I conjured the hospital's blanched-white walls, machines, and bags of drugs over and over in my mind's eye. Clutching the pillows to my chest, I gasped for air and tried to control the wracking waves of anguish. I wanted more than anything for the entire nightmare to vanish and for it all to be untrue, for it to be a terrible mistake. But it wasn't. I had cancer, though I didn't know yet what kind, which was another nightmare. I would have to slog my way through treatment one way or another. It was one of the two darkest moments of the journey.

Sometime during my treatment, I received a card that I have kept until this day. It has a photograph of the bow of a sailboat amid rough seas under cloudy skies, taken from the perspective of the helm. Quoting Daniel Achinsky, it reads, "Only in the storm can you see the art of a real sailor." It's true. I thought I knew who I was: a determined individual who got whatever I wanted as long as I set my mind to it. That's what my mother had always taught me. But never, *never*, had I been confronted with the challenges that lay before me with cancer treatment. What came forth from deep within me was strength I never knew I had. Whether it was ingrained or taught, I don't know. But it was there, and within days I had set my course: I would fight.

It took a few days to find out that I had stage four ovarian cancer. My odd relief at this news was unexpected. I had known someone who died from stomach cancer, and it was more fearful to me than ovarian, although ovarian has quite a bad rap. It's not something you want to spend much time reading about on the Internet, I quickly learned. But at my first meeting with Dr. Hufford—"the Huff," as I soon nicknamed him—he told me it was treatable and beatable. With that I knew I had found a teammate who would support me along the way and get me out the other side of the journey's long tunnel. I spent many days interviewing and researching other physicians and hospitals, but none of them had the Huff's positive outlook. I stuck with him because he thought the same way I did.

Like me, the Huff also had cancer. Yet he was a happy and good-natured man and as filled with a zest for life as anyone I'd ever known. He was *living* with cancer, and so would I. Having cancer was inconvenient to be sure, but it wasn't the end. There still was life, and plenty of it, to be lived, although in a far different way than had been lived before.

After breaking the news to Andrea, there was Erika, my best friend and ally. I had to tell her, too. But how? With the deepest dread, I picked up the phone to invite her over for a glass of wine the evening after the Huff confirmed my diagnosis.

Andrea was with me when Erika arrived, and I popped open a magnum of my favorite champagne, which I'd been saving for a special occasion. This was the starting point of my change: Stop saving things. Stop saving that great bottle of wine for a better reason to open it. Stop waiting. Stop postponing things until a later time that might be better or more suitable. If you can, enjoy it now. There is an old cliché about having no guarantee of tomorrow. I was now intimately aware of what that meant; without realizing it, I had already shifted my ability to live in and enjoy the present.

"Sit down, take a load off." I invited Erika over to the couch.

"What's the occasion? Is everything okay?" she asked, knowing something was amiss before I said a word.

I walked into the living room, champagne glasses in hand, and poured us all a round of her favorite, Roederer L'Ermitage. She sipped it, then smiled.

"That'll do, pig," she said as she always did when something pleased her. It was an old line from a delightful movie about a sheep-herding pig that wins the day after a lifetime of being the underdog (pun intended). I'd always liked that movie.

I sat down next to her and looked at her squarely. Her next sip stopped in midair. She stared at me, her eyes open in that wide way that happens when shock and surprise come all at once.

"Oh no," she whispered. "Oh God no!" louder this time, then she began to cry and took me in her arms.

We cried together then, rocking back and forth, our pain, past and present, combined. Beyond my own fear, I was deeply sorry to put her through another foray with cancer, this time with her best friend.

Erika took the news badly, and the evening was dark for her. I knew she feared the worst, so the next day I made a special trip to her house to discuss the plan for my treatment. I was very, very clear that I needed her on my team. I needed her strength. I needed her love. I needed her positive attitude. And I promised her that with her help, I would defeat this disease.

And she knew I delivered on my promises.

Overexposed

REFLECTIONS

THIS MORNING, I AWAKENED TO AN E-MAIL IN MY INBOX, A MESSAGE from the American Cancer Society asking me to "tell my story." *Weird*, I think. *Almost like a hint from the universe.* As I begin to read it, I am confronted by someone's tale of surviving Hodgkin's lymphoma three times. I stop. I skip ahead to learn the purpose of the website he is touting. I reread the subject line of the e-mail again, and I find my iPad to jot down this note of advice for an unknown audience: don't overexpose yourself to cancer.

What do I mean?

At the beginning of my treatment, several people suggested that I join a support group. For many, this is exactly the right choice. Don't get me wrong, I think support groups can serve a very useful purpose, and many people get great benefits from such groups. But they're not for me. I was utterly disinterested in sitting in a room filled with people battling cancer and listening to their frightening stories. I was already too afraid, and I didn't need anyone else's experience to load on top of my own. I avoid scary movies because my active imagination makes me relive the scary parts again and again for weeks thereafter. So instead of focusing on my cancer, I chose to just go on living my life as I always had—spending time with friends, going to dance class, riding my bicycle. I never joined a group of any kind. I chose to focus on life and kept my focus on cancer to a minimum.

This topic came up at one point during my treatment when Andrea and I had a conversation about various ways to deal with the situation.

"You know, I've heard that outcomes are better for people who join support groups," she said, trying to be helpful.

"What?" I was incredulous. "Are you suggesting that if I don't join a support group my outcome won't be good? You make it sound like I'm putting myself at risk by not joining a group. That's ridiculous," I scoffed.

"I'm not saying that." She tried to right the boat. "It's just that there are studies out there showing that people in groups have very positive outcomes, that's all."

But I didn't want to hear it. I knew what I needed to hear, and though it was an exercise in language management, no doubt, it was what I needed at the time.

"Look," I pleaded, "I don't need you to question my treatment outcome. Instead, every time I say I'm scared or worried or concerned about whether chemo is the right thing to do, just tell me everything will be okay, even if you don't believe it."

I needed encouragement, 110 percent encouragement, at all times. If she had fears of her own about my condition, I asked her to please share them with her own support circle—her friends and family—but not with me. After all, I was the one heading to cancer's front line. The only thing I absolutely wanted or needed was to be told that it was all going to be okay.

Funny, how life is. I learned much later, after we ended our relationship, that my request had helped sever our bond because she believed she wasn't able to express herself fully to me. Perhaps she was right. All I know is that, when the whole ordeal began and I was an anxious, frightened ovarian-cancer patient, I was desperately trying to manage my information intake. Support, *positive* support, was what I needed. I could barely manage my own fear, let alone handle anyone else's.

But that's the way this disease is sometimes. It forces you to look deep inside yourself and get what you need to go forward. Sometimes what you need is not something others can give. Sometimes others cannot handle it; sometimes they can. You just never know. But what I do know is that, to this day, I still avoid listening to other people's cancer stories, joining groups to discuss it, or otherwise becoming engaged with cancer or its topics. Maybe it's just my own fear because I don't want to be one of those multi-cancer survivors. I don't want to have to go through that war again. Once was plenty; believe me. It's easier to do battle the first time because you have no real idea what the battlefield looks like. But once you've been through it, the idea of repeating the process all over again is most overwhelming.

Friends

MARCH 2011

I ALREADY MENTIONED ONE OTHER THING I LEARNED AT THE
onset of this process: you find out pretty quickly who your real
friends are. People you've known for decades will fade into the
woodwork without so much as a card or phone call. But people you
consider mere acquaintances will step up to the plate, and not only
will they swing, they'll hit a home run. That was the unexpected
blessing of this disease. At fifty-one years old, I knew absolutely
who my true friends were, without doubt. That knowledge made it
easier to let go of the unhealthy relationships in my life and those
people with whom my connection was not what I once thought
it was.

Take, for example, my relationship with Darin. He had been a
friend of mine for more than thirty years. We met when I was still in
college, we moved cross-country together, shared an apartment, and
remained friends as the decades flew by. Long after we no longer lived
in close proximity, any time we got together we would pick up exactly
where we left off as if no time at all had passed. But as the geographic
distance grew between us, we saw less and less of one another. Promising
for years he would come to California for a visit, he finally made good
on his word and came out just weeks before the news broke. Weeks.

And as always, we enjoyed good times while he was here, not skipping a beat from where we were before.

Then something odd happened. After I was diagnosed, I never heard his voice again. Not a word. I received the occasional comment to a blog post and an e-mail or two, but he never called me. Sure, I could have picked up the phone myself, but I was so mired in my own medical chaos that I didn't think about it. My other close friends called, and quickly! They wanted to check in. They wanted to offer support. They wanted to visit and help me. But not Darin.

I thought about this for a long while, and also did some reading on the topic. It turns out that people don't always react to a cancer diagnosis of a friend or loved one as you might imagine or hope. Rather, they tend to gravitate toward one of two camps. First, they may disengage completely from your life because the pain of losing you would be too great. They unconsciously decide "she's going to die anyway," so they try and distance themselves from the pain before it actually happens. They may also disengage out of fear—fear of their own mortality. Cancer remains a big, scary proposition for most of us. There are limited cures despite the billions of dollars we pour into research. It takes time to find a cure, and some of us have more time than others. But knowing someone with cancer brings the point too close to home for many, and they simply run away.

If you find yourself facing a similar problem, know you are not alone. Unfortunately, it happens all too often. But rather than focus on those who might disappear from your life, focus on the friends you've gained and the friendships that have proven to be real and enduring.

And So It Began ...

APRIL 2011

I WAS SCHEDULED FOR A COMPLETE HYSTERECTOMY TO REMOVE THE cancerous ovaries, which thankfully went off without a hitch. What should have taken three hours only took ninety minutes. Thanks to Erika, the size of my unwelcome tumor was announced over the Internet in one of her first (and last!) medical updates to friends and family:

April 5, 2011

... I don't know if this constitutes a record but almost thirty-six hours after being wheeled into surgery, The Mockster is heading home!!! TONIGHT!!!

... The tumor the docs removed turned out to be the size of a generous Texas Ruby Red grapefruit (and for you non-Texans, that is one big piece of fruit, and if you don't eat them, you should because they are not only delicious, but really high in good fiber. (Message provided by the Texas Grapefruit Council!)

The results of the tumor biopsy will be known next week. In the meantime, the lead singer of this band is going to recuperate, relax, and get back to telling us roadies what to do.

More updates from the "Mockster Tour" will be posted in the next day or so.

Thank you to all of you for keeping that positive energy flowing this way … you are some powerful people!!!

Hugs!
Erika

I had shunned a site on Caring Bridge kindly created by one of my friends—"All those people die, don't they?" I had lamented—and instead set up my own private blog for those who cared to follow along. I chose for the cover photo a picture of me apparently hanging from a ledge by my fingertips, taken during my fiftieth birthday trip to Sedona, Arizona:

The site, dubbed themockster.blogspot.com, referenced a nickname foisted upon me like an old ox yoke many years ago. The following line announced my marching orders:

> A swollen lymph node in my neck led me to an early diagnosis of ovarian cancer. But wait! All is well. It is eminently treatable and beatable. The journey begins now. Thanks so much for all your love and support.

Caring Bridge be damned.

Little more than a week after open abdominal surgery I was back in dance class, with the flattest stomach I'd had in years. I don't recommend surgery as an alternative to weight loss, but gee whiz—at fifty-one—I was the envy of the twenty-five-year-olds. Of course, I was also seven pounds lighter, and that isn't a good thing when you're five foot nine and less than 130 pounds. I looked like a string bean, and not in a good way.

Having been an athlete all my life—I later learned the term "lifetime athlete" from medical articles and doctors—I continued my fitness program after the surgery with a renewed effort. I wanted to be in the best possible shape before starting chemotherapy.

My diet changed. I exercised every single day. I meditated each morning. I saw friends and made plans. I went to the office, though infrequently. I shopped at the farmers' market and made fresh meals with organic foods. I stopped using my microwave oven and jettisoned the plastic water bottles that had been part of my life for too long. As advised by my nutritionist, I took handfuls of vitamins and minerals each day to build and boost my system for the coming onslaught. Fiber. Exercise. Health. My focus turned to the most basic of all our instincts: survival. I would be ready for the jungle warfare that cancer was bringing to my doorstep.

Perhaps life had already prepared me for this journey, because it certainly wasn't the first time that I had adopted a take-no-prisoner's attitude. I dropped out of college at twenty with only seventeen credit hours of elective classes remaining. I thought my mother would kill me. Ignoring her sage advice to stay enrolled and get my degree, I moved halfway across the country and worked for ten years at random jobs before finally going back to school. It took two years of night classes while working full-time to get that undergraduate degree, a prerequisite for law school, which I finally began at the age of thirty. Determined to get a decent job, I concentrated fiercely on every book, every class, and every project, and graduated in the top ten of my class— not 10 percent, the *top ten students*. It made my mother proud. Finally.

There was an obvious pattern of diligence in my past, which I put to good use with the whole cancer thing. And the beauty of keeping busy as you prepare for cancer treatment is that, well, you're busy. But at some point the research and the reading and the girding of loins stops, and you're left with just your thoughts.

A couple of weeks following surgery, the second of the two dark moments came; it felt not so much like a dark cloud hovering overhead, but rather like I was being crushed by a giant rock. And thus arose the name of one of my first blog entries, which unveiled the emotional underpinnings of my cancer diagnosis:

April 16, 2011: The Giant Rock

Yesterday was chock-full-o-docs, and not in a good way. I'll spare you the gory details, but suffice it to say the information overload felt like drinking from a fire hose. There were few surprises: Both doctors recommended identical chemotherapies, though one hospital offers a couple of clinical trials that involve lower doses of the drugs on a weekly basis as opposed to higher doses every three weeks. While I had once harbored a secret notion that all was so much better now that the surgery was complete, and that I could forestall treatment until after my long-awaited vacation in June, my notion was dispelled. I was unaware until yesterday that treatment needs to begin six to eight weeks following surgery because, now that the cancer cells are royally "pissed off," they are replicating and dividing. The chemotherapy works by attacking and killing the cells while they are in their active state.

My other secretly held notion—that I might spend some time trying holistic treatments first, and then turn to chemotherapy only as a last resort if that doesn't work— was dispelled for the same reason. Waiting beyond the six- to eight-week window is ill advised because the cells slow down their dividing action by that time, and the chemo is less effective.

Oh yeah, and then there was all the scary chatter about the aggressive nature of my cancer and the low survival rates, though I was assured that women in my age group and with my "performance profile" (i.e., fitness level) generally do better. I awoke this morning feeling like I was lying under a giant rock and cannot get out of bed.

Confronting one's own mortality is exhausting.

I will eventually get up, put on the gloves, and start swinging, and I look forward to that moment. But right now, in this moment, I feel overwhelmed.

There comes a point in every terrible scenario that life presents us when we succumb to being overwhelmed by it all. Sometimes—not only with cancer, but with many other things—it just becomes too much to handle. There is something to be said for doing the deep dive into an emotional abyss during those times. One of my dear friends says that she feels the most alive in those moments of despair and utter sadness. It makes her feel completely human. She's right, in ways that I didn't really appreciate or understand before. It's a rare moment when we're attuned to the very humanness of ourselves. Our mortality. To what we actually *feel* about things, and the tenuous nature of our very existence.

Not long after my "Giant Rock" post, I dried my eyes, took a deep breath, and shuffled back toward that long-trodden path with which I was so familiar: my life before cancer came calling.

I managed to drag myself out of the house and into the sunshine, put the top down on the car, and drove to dance class. Just getting outside and into the fresh air was a positive perspective changer. And though I was obviously not fit enough for a two-hour workout—having had major surgery only ten days earlier—I did stay for the entire class because it was a joy to see my classmates and friends. My beloved instructor shouted a hearty "Jan's back!" that prompted a little hurrah from my buddies and brought a smile to my face and tears to my eyes. It was a relief to reconnect with my "ideal life" once again.

My "ideal life" was a concept I created many years ago after I read *The Passion Test* by Janet Bray Attwood and Chris Attwood. The book guides you to think about what really matters and what you want in life, and to create a mantra around those things to bring them to fruition. Hocus pocus? Maybe. Self-brainwashing? Possibly. Nothing to lose by doing it? Definitely. Over the years I created and regularly repeated this mantra on good health: *I am happy and grateful to be living my ideal life, by enjoying perfect health and taking care of my body, and being outdoors.* These were things that were important to me and on which I placed both a conscious and subconscious focus.

Now, presented with this latest challenge, I figured I might as well get back to basics and stay focused on what I wanted for myself: perfect health. Returning to dance class was one way to redirect my thinking toward the solution rather than the problem.

A drawing made for me by my dance instructor,
Alan. Illustration courtesy of Alan Scofield.

The Hair

APRIL 2011

ONCE I TURNED MY FULL ATTENTION TO SOLVING THE PROBLEM, I started investigating which doctor and hospital would provide me with the best treatment plan. Two were in the running: California Pacific Medical Center (CPMC) and University of California at San Francisco (UCSF). I was amazed and surprised to learn that both hospitals have adjunct facilities that focus exclusively on holistic patient care. Acupuncture, massage, yoga, and wellness nutrition were just some of their nontraditional offerings. The facilities were beautiful, and the resources were more than I would have ever imagined.

I made an appointment at the women's clinic near CPMC, with a nurse practitioner who handled cases involving breast and gynecological cancers. I'm not sure what I had in mind—probably to ask questions about the doctors or the facilities—but the visit marked another turning point.

The practitioner launched into a recital of all the things that I might encounter during treatment. First, there was the treatment itself, the hours-long intravenous infusion of chemicals, one after the other. Each treatment would take at least six hours, with six visits spaced three weeks apart. Possible side effects included nausea, loss of appetite, and vomiting. I would definitely be tired because I'd lose so many red blood cells and would probably need a lot of rest. My immune system would be compromised from losing white blood cells. She talked about my cancer antigen score (CA-125), a test for the protein typically found in high amounts in the blood of patients with ovarian cancer. Mine was over 3,000, well beyond the normal 0–35 range. I was overwhelmed by the influx of information, and yet I felt oddly removed from the situation, as if we were talking about someone else.

Among other things, she assured me I would lose my hair. Taxol and Carboplatin—two drugs that kill ovarian cancer cells—cause hair loss.

"But wait a minute," I said. "I've heard from others, including my own brother, that people's individual bodies react differently to the drugs and that some people don't lose their hair at all."

Of course, I never focused on this before I was diagnosed. I had no reason to do so. Like others, I dismissed the notion with a wave of the hand and pronounced that if I ever had cancer, I would just go bald. Yet now, here I was. Sitting in a nurse's office, hearing a parade of horribles and facing head on the prospect of my life as a cancer patient.

"It's the drugs," she began. "The drugs themselves are what dictate hair loss. Not all of them destroy the hair follicle, which is what causes the hair to fall out. But these do."

Then she told me where I could get a wig, compliments of the American Cancer Society.

I don't know what it was she said that drove me over the edge. But something did. I suddenly realized I couldn't breathe. My chest tightened. I was losing it and desperately needed to get out of there. Tears welled in my eyes.

I looked directly at her and said, "Not me. I will not lose my hair." And with that, I got up and left her office. I did not see here again for more than a year; when I returned to say hello and proudly display my full head of hair.

As my mother could have told her, you just don't tell me I can't do something. That's just bait. In such event, I will exercise my best efforts to prove you wrong.

About the hair, here's the deal: I quickly realized it wasn't about vanity. It was about wellness. That was the very core of my focus, and the Huff fully supported me. My plan was to continue living my life as normal, fitting in those pesky cancer treatments as scheduled. I would act normally, do normal things, and—focused on wellness—heal myself and keep my body healthy throughout the treatment. Part of that program was to experience the face I saw in the mirror each morning and dealing with the reactions of others. Yep, people react to you in ways you never imagined when you have cancer. Believe me. But I was determined to limit all negativity and pity as much as humanly possible. Keeping my hair did that for me.

Penguin Cold Caps is a company that was formed in the United Kingdom almost two decades ago. The nurse practitioner from whose office I ran mentioned these caps offhandedly (and without encouragement), but Erika later told me that one of her friends had used them successfully during breast-cancer treatment. I began investigating, talking to other women who had used the caps with great success, and decided to try them. What did I have to lose except, of course, my hair?

The basic premise is that the caps freeze your scalp during the infusion of the chemo cocktail to prevent the hair follicle from absorbing the deadly drugs.

Sure enough, my hair, though it thinned somewhat, remained virtually intact throughout the treatments. Each morning I got up, looked in the mirror, and saw a healthy person, not a cancer patient. It was weird enough when my eyebrows and eyelashes finally fell out, but eyebrows I could color in with a pencil, and new eyelashes could be glued on. The hair on my head, however, was my internal and external symbol of normalcy. Not once did I stand in line at the coffee shop under pitying glances. Never was I forced to hear perfect strangers lament my case, sharing with me their own stories about some dead relative lost to cancer. In a spinning world, I had managed to control some part of my own environment and the incoming messages to my psyche. It was a wonderful aspect of my treatment that I would do all over again if I had to.

But then there was the wig.

As a lawyer, I'd learned long ago to expect the unexpected and cover all bases to the fullest extent possible. I figured I'd better go see that wig lady just in case this Penguin Cap thing didn't work out. So off I went.

On a quiet corner in San Rafael stood a nondescript building with a nondescript name that provided comfort and self-esteem to women who are struggling with cancer or some other debilitating illness. It turns out that the wig lady not only sold wigs, she also sold prostheses for breast cancer patients.

After running around to keep up with my cancer to-do list, I found myself sitting quietly on a low, soft couch in a dimly lit room, waiting for the nice lady with the wigs to come out and greet me. Her previous client was just leaving, a short woman with salt-and-pepper hair who appeared to be in her mid-sixties, holding a new bag of boobs.

I glanced at the woman, then away, and caught myself holding back tears. Then, responding to a greeting directed to me, I followed my host into her secret room of headdresses and trusses.

Oh the wigs! There were hundreds of them, everywhere, and of every size, shape, and color. Except mine, of course; I had shoulder-length, blonde, curly hair. Most wigs don't come that way. Most are straight hair, whether synthetic or real, long or short. I learned for the first time about Philippine girls who sell their hair to wig makers. Their wigs—luxurious rivers of silky black ink—are the most expensive. I opted instead for a synthetic wig that was provided to me free of charge because I was a cancer patient. One was too blonde; the other a coppery red. *Red! Why not shake it up a bit?* But when I was left alone for a moment to decide between the two, the tears came again. There I was, alone in a room filled with wigs for cancer patients, and wearing one. *I had cancer.* It was another of those unpleasant reality checks that occur with some frequency following a cancer diagnosis. Finally, grateful for one of cancer's first obvious perks but certain I wouldn't really lose my hair, I picked the too-blonde, just-in-case wig that made me look like a rock star. Well, sort of. I probably would have been more convincing as a rocker if I'd picked the fire-engine-red one, which was very Vegas, baby.

Wig in hand, the following week, Erika and I headed down to the South Bay to find the woman who would style my new wig to make it look like my own hair. Yeah, right.

The house was in a hodgepodge of a neighborhood somewhere near Pacifica. Access to the "beauty shop" was gained through a side door to the garage, where we were welcomed by stacks and stacks of stuff: laundry, old shoes, plastic bottles, newspapers—the general riff-raff one might find in anyone's garage, except maybe more of it. A gangly teenage boy buzzed about, asking for money, or car keys, or both. There were a few wigs here and there, not nearly the assortment at the wig lady's shop, but I had brought my own. All I needed her to do was cut and style it and make it look like my hair.

Well, that was not to be. As I said earlier, wigs do not come in shoulder-length, curly blonde hair.

"But I can perm it," she offered, less than enthusiastically.

Having survived the 1970s the first time, I was utterly disinterested in a headful of permanent wave ringlets framing my fifty-one-year-old face. Thanks, but no thanks. I would live with it straight; just add some bangs, please. After a few snips here and there, Erika and I were on our way back to the city. I tried it on in the car just for fun, with sunglasses. We had a laugh at its ridiculousness and my rock-star profile, but then the tears threatened to drop from behind my Hollywood shades. I tried to suck it up and get on with the next step. A good friend and a quick hug were all I needed to regroup and get the show on the road.

Choices

MAY 2011

IF YOU'VE EVER BEEN UNEMPLOYED, EVEN FOR A BRIEF SPELL, YOU'LL recognize the feeling I'm about to describe: nowhere to go, no particular time to get there. It's a weird feeling of floating around without purpose. You don't know what to do with your newfound free time. All your friends are going about their daily routines, the world keeps spinning, and you float around looking out from the bubble in which you feel captured.

For me, that was only part of the story. I was in a bubble all right, but rather than feeling like I had nothing to do, I was firmly focused on interviewing physicians; visiting hospitals and treatment facilities; and meeting with nutritionists, acupuncturists, and others to determine how best to work my way out of this very bad situation. The one thing I continued to avoid was surfing the Internet. The occasional success story was buried so far down in the search results that I couldn't read through the tears once I did find it. I gave up and assigned that grueling task to Andrea. It's no wonder she grew sullen as the days and weeks passed.

One of cancer's many side effects is a feeling of complete helplessness. Cancer has a way of making you feel totally out of control because, as it turns out, you are. The act of interviewing doctors and visiting hospitals gives one the illusion of having control over something—that, and the frozen hair, of course. It gave me the sense that I had some choice over how this would all play out, over what would happen, over the outcome. Of course, it's just a roll of the dice, but I figured if I went at it full bore, as I had with most things in life, I might succeed in beating it.

Interviewing medical personnel and touring facilities was an eye-opening experience, sometimes not in a good way. As my blog and journal entries reveal, one of the more difficult days was spent visiting one doctor at a hospital I didn't choose, who used most of our time together reciting the very low statistics on successful outcomes. He also told me to cancel my long awaited fall trip to Barcelona, which I'd be visiting for the first time, and get serious about this life-threatening disease. Feeling as if I had been beaten, I struggled to breathe as the elevator took Andrea and me down to the lobby level, where I practically ran out of the hospital, away from the pale walls and fluorescent lighting, aching for fresh air and to feel the sun on my face. Right then it hit me: *I was probably going to die. Really die.* Not at some unknown time or from some unknown thing. No, I would probably die from ovarian cancer, and sooner rather than later.

Choking back tears is a hard thing to do, which you know if you've ever tried it. It feels like you are smothering yourself. Your entire being seems ready to explode as your breath comes in gasps and the tears rush forth behind your eyes. It's overwhelming. But the tears finally spilled once I made it through the glass doors. I stood on the sidewalk, not caring if people stared, and wept. Then I wept some more. Andrea put her arm around me and steadied me to the car, then took me home and put me to bed. There I stayed for hours and hours, covers over my head, not daring to come out lest I be faced with a reality I couldn't bear.

But like a terrible storm before the calm, crisp stillness that follows, this dark period passed and left me facing a new day with renewed purpose. I would do something different. I would find some way to combat this killer without poisoning myself with chemo. My relentless search began again:

> Perhaps acupuncture? That would work, right? Or Qigong, an Eastern practice of movement and enlightenment similar to Tai Chi that was unknown to me but somehow seemed different. Meditation? Great idea. What about yoga? And drinking juiced vegetables definitely would fix it, wouldn't it?

I tried all of these and everything else I could think of during the period between my surgery and the date chemotherapy was set to begin. But chemo claimed the marquee because my little cancer cells had metastasized to my lymph system and beat a path all the way up my core, resulting in the lump I had first noticed near my collarbone. My cancer could be eradicated only with chemicals, not a knife, and not anything else.

Ultimately, I settled on what I knew with certainty would be useful: a continuing fitness regime that would keep my body strong over the coming weeks. The Huff also recommended exercise, so I continued riding my bicycle almost daily to create the oxygenated environment that hopefully would stop further growth of the cancer cells. Only later would I learn how right we were, and how much my commitment to fitness aided my recovery.

I found a nutritionist to prepare my body for the rigor of it all. Good foods, vitamins, minerals, and smoothies became part of my daily routine. I found an acupuncturist whose treatments helped boost my immune system. Although I desperately dreaded chemo, I was in good spirits and fixated on integrative health and wellness tools to carry me forward over the coming weeks and months. But I was still not completely sold on the chemotherapy path; it seemed like such a drastic measure, and I feared the toll it would take on my body and my overall health. In fact, I considered not doing it at all.

As my date with the cancer center drew closer, I pleaded with the universe for a cure that would spare me from poisoning myself with drugs. I talked to a therapist. I had massages. I went to yoga and Qigong and acupuncture. I meditated and held healing stones and chanted. I would have drunk squid ink. I read and made inquiries and, eventually, searched the Internet myself for a cure. Nothing convinced my lawyer mind that anything short of surgery and chemo would have any real or lasting effect on killing the beast within. Finally, and reluctantly, I concluded that only chemotherapy would stem the tide of the growing cells.

The days ticked down toward the first of my six treatments. Regrettably, and with some sense of defeat, I cancelled my planned trip abroad. More than a drop of bitterness flavored my corresponding blog post:

May 9, 2011: Don't Cry for Me, Barcelona

I just cancelled a long-awaited windjammer cruise from Barcelona to Rome next month. Much harder than I thought to give this up for some stupid cancer. As if having the stupid cancer isn't bad enough … I mean, really? Forfeit my trip? This sucks. (Do try and resist the urge to post a comment about how "there will always be other trips.")

With just days to go, I opted for a girl's day out and enjoyed a brand-new hairdo that I was committed to preserving over the coming weeks; the "safety wig" was tucked away in my closet. Giving a nod to the Italian language I am so fond of, this post followed my trip to the salon:

———————————— ✤ ————————————

May 13, 2011: *Belli Capelli* (loosely translated, it means "nice hair")

Just showing off my last haircut for awhile in this official "before" picture. The Penguin Caps arrived today and are currently taking up 90 percent of my freezer space. Andrea has graciously accepted the role and responsibility for maintaining my curls *au naturale.*

———————————— ✤ ————————————

The Huff scheduled my first chemo round for May 25, 2011, at the Bryan Hemming Cancer Center. As cancer treatment facilities go, this one was pretty remarkable. Recently remodeled, it was still shiny and new when I went to check it out. All patients were provided a private, spacious room with a flat-screen television (which I never watched), a comfy big reclining chair (in which I spent all of my time), and friendly and capable nurses (whom I came to both fear and admire). I spent six days there, each day coming three weeks after the last. All in all, I was in and out of that place for a little more than three months.

I would be lying if I said I wasn't scared. I was. The very thought of needles shoved in my already-thin arms was more than I could stand. When you add the fact that those needless would be loaded with platinum and tree bark, well, it wasn't a pleasant thought. I doubt it is for anyone.

I had received an avalanche of information during the previous weeks, but I finally managed to dig myself out from under it, make some sense of it, and formulate what I believed was a successful plan with an exceptional team. A huge chunk of the project was keeping a good frame of reference and trying not to panic.

At that point in the journey there was nothing left to do but buck up and keep moving forward. It's amazing what you can do when you have little choice in the matter.

On a Clear Day

MAY 25, 2011

THE FIRST ROUND OF CHEMO CAME ON THE PROVERBIAL CLEAR DAY IN May. Two giant coolers of dry ice filled with Penguin Caps in tow, Andrea, Erika, and I made our way to the cancer center. I can no longer recount the details of that day, thanks to about thirty milligrams of liquid Benadryl, but I remember being immensely glad it was over.

Thankfully, only two photos were taken to document the adventure, one of me waiting for the drugs, and one with my frozen head:

May 25, 2011: Are We Having Fun Yet?

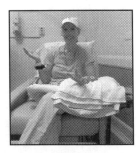

All hooked up and waiting for the pharmacy to send the bazookas and flamethrowers down here.

May 25, 2011: Bring on the Caps

We are on board and Andrea is working furiously to get the caps organized. Hair freezing. Yeah!

If you've never encased your head in ice, you do not know how cold subzero can be. It's cold   really, really cold. I can't recommend it as something to try just for fun, but those unattractive turbans were terribly effective in freezing my hair follicles. A half hour before the first drug was infused, on went the cap, which had been frozen in dry ice down to a chilly forty-two degrees below zero. The first one is the worst because your head is still at room temperature, but the Benadryl kept the pain in check. Barely. The caps then are rotated every thirty minutes for the duration of the entire infusion, plus two more hours after it ends as your body continues to metabolize the drugs. It is a tedious process to keep your head frozen: the caps are rotated on and off, one by one, each one colder than the last. You need good friends to help because you can't do it alone.

The complicated part about using them was the schlepping of dry ice to each and every treatment, but a very dear friend graciously donated a hospital-grade freezer to the cancer center so that I could conveniently store my caps on-site. Unfortunately, the freezer didn't arrive before my last round of chemo, but it remains there to this day for other hair-saving cancer patients. His generous gift was just another wonderful surprise that cancer brought into my life—experiencing firsthand the unlimited generosity and kindness of others. There were unexpected blessings at every turn.

All in all, round one was a success and just like my favorite kind of airplane flight: on time and uneventful. I was not allergic to any of the medications, and my drug-induced state helped me sleep away most of the day (much to the chagrin of my teammates Erika and Andrea, who for eight hours endured the minute-by-minute action changing my Penguin Caps required). The day ended with my head thawing and a face-plant on my pillow.

Oddly enough, I usually felt pretty good the day after a treatment. I chalked it up to the steroid high, from which I would plummet on the second and third day afterward.

On the first day following round one, I was enjoying a taste of spring during a little outing in my car with the top down, when I was pulled over by a policeman for doing a "California roll" through a stop sign.

The traffic stop, which pre-C would have been a mere annoyance, felt like a slap. Although I was out and about, I was still not myself, adjusting to my new sea legs of the cancer treatment voyage. Like a wave, the internalized upset I was feeling bubbled to the surface. It was that feeling we often have when one thing piles on top of another and we ask ourselves, "Now what? What *else* can happen?"

Before the officer could write out the ticket, I blurted out, "Can you please not give that to me? I just started chemo yesterday."

To my surprise, his pen stood still. He looked at me, snapped closed his ticket book, and pushed his glasses on top of his head.

"You know," he said. "I can understand about the chemo. I'll let it slide this time. Take care of yourself." Then he walked away.

"See?" I laughed out loud to Andrea, who was along for the ride. "Cancer is good for something after all."

She was not amused. But as quickly as a hummingbird changes direction, I did too. I thought I had left mood swings far behind when mid-life came calling. But as if having cancer isn't fun enough, the drugs allowed me to enjoy those mood swings all over again. Random as it seemed, I found my humor in it all. Lesson one: fighting cancer requires a good sense of humor.

A little-known fact, at least to me, was that modern medicine had invented an injection called Neulasta, which was designed to offset the white-cell-killing effects of the chemotherapy and keep patients from becoming autoimmune (and thus susceptible to every bug and germ in sight). That's the good news. The bad news is that it is a ridiculously expensive drug that insurance companies hate to pay for, so a battle ensued about whether I needed it or not. The other bad news is that it transformed me much the same way Bill Bixby turned into the Incredible Hulk, only with the flu. At least that's what it felt like. The joint and bone pain was just shy of intolerable and left me in bed or on the couch sleeping for a day and a half. Eventually, time and Advil brought me back around to the land of the living. Being a control freak of sorts, I found my lack of control over the medications or their effects on my body a tough pill to swallow.

Back to rule number 1: a sense of humor. It's a must have. Seriously. If I couldn't find something remotely funny about my circumstances, then I might as well just lie down and die.

"Funny" is relative, of course. There are many, many moments of *not* funny, moments during which it is impossible to find anything funny. I chose not to dwell on those moments and instead to look on the bright side of the madness. But what was the bright side? A perspective change, that's what. As the days passed, my perspective on life—indeed, on living— changed. I began to look forward to those blessedly mundane days at the office, when I tried to make myself useful to my law-firm partners and clients. The rut in which I walked every day took on a whole new brightness; it was a rut no more.

A Plug for the Bicycle

REFLECTIONS

I've been doing this bicycle thing now for about twenty-five years. It's hard to believe so much time has passed since I bought that twenty-five-dollar Huffy 10-speed from the Salvation Army. After riding for a year in various road rallies—usually, you pay a fee and get a free water bottle—or around the neighborhood, I decided it wasn't a fad, so I bought myself a new Bianchi Prima. That was twenty-four years ago.

It was black with red pin striping, which I thought was the cat's pajamas. I rode that chromoly-framed beauty for ten years and never glanced at another, until one day I was in my favorite bike store in Richardson, Texas. A sleek, silvery, titanium Bianchi with a mega-size aero-shaped down-tube caught my eye. It was love at first sight (or first ride, if you count the little spin I took around the inside of that Texas-sized bike shop). My black beauty went to a good friend who was doing his first multi-day fundraising ride, and my new silvery titanium took her rightful place of honor in my house. She was an absolute favorite.

The thing about bike riding, I find, is that it pays big benefits. Surging downhill at perilous speed with the wind whipping my face feels like flying. Hill climbing shoves blood through my heart and legs as the pedals surge round and round; it is all so invigorating, so healthy.

The flood of endorphins that follows is like a drug. I love all of it, and riding was a mainstay throughout my cancer treatment.

The other thing about biking, though, is its meditative effect. A therapist friend of mine once described something called TFT (Thought Field Therapy), which is a way to break an emotional dam when one gets stuck. It's frequently used to treat people suffering from posttraumatic stress disorder. The pedaling of a bicycle is much the same: the constant up-and-down motion is almost hypnotic. I have laughed, cried, and thought big thoughts while riding my bicycle. I've worked my way into and out of relationships. I've reached hard decisions that I couldn't get my head around earlier. I've had epiphanies and learning moments. I've seen things I would not otherwise have seen. I have enjoyed. I have lived. Bike riding has become like a drug to me over the years, and if I don't get out for a ride on a pretty regular basis, I can get pretty grumpy.

Many people have a similar fitness addiction, whether it's swimming, running, or playing tennis. There is something about that mind/body connection that just can't be emulated through reading books or watching television. It's a way to calibrate your health that also provides a window to the spiritual aspects of your life.

After many years spent with friends wondering why in the world we get up early in the morning to pound up hill after hill just for fun, riding revealed itself as a reward after my diagnosis. My lifelong love of fitness provided a strong foundation for my body to fight the cancer and tolerate the chemotherapy treatments.

I can't tell you how many people said to me, "You look amazing! I cannot believe you're in cancer treatment. No one would ever know." I attribute their amazement in large part to my fitness. A big part of my treatment and recovery program was to exercise every day. I did core workouts and free weights at home several days a week. I went for walks with my five-pound, black and cuddly bundle of Chihuahua cuteness, Zorro. And I would ride. I would get on that bicycle and ride. Ten, twenty, thirty miles—however far I felt I could go. It kept me grounded in my *real* life, if you will, and reminded me that I had a strong body that could beat this disease. I refused to be compromised or stopped by the treatment, which to me, was a nuisance. A big, fat, awful nuisance. I did my best to continue living as I always had, but fitness was my focus, and I was diligent about it.

Because chemo kills practically every red and white blood cell in your body, along with the cancer cells, over the course of eighteen weeks my red count got lower and lower until I started fainting. Finally, after my second-to-last treatment, the Huff told me I needed either a Procrit injection or a blood transfusion.

"Ah ha! Finally I can do some blood doping," I joked. But my red count was so far in the toilet that the Procrit only took me to the low end of normal. There was no big boost for cycling. Later, my blood-doping joke became less funny when the world turned its attention to the very real pollution of the professional side of my beloved sport.

Those last few weeks of treatment were really difficult, not only because the overall degradation of my red blood cells made it hard to even walk up a flight of stairs, but because I couldn't ride my bike. I couldn't enjoy the exhilaration of flying downhill, or seeing my feathered companions, the cranes and pelicans that flew alongside at the water's edge where I rode. I missed the flowers, the sky. I missed my little freedom getaways. As a substitute, I stayed outside by taking more and longer walks with Zorro and with friends. The great outdoors was where it was for me, and that remained a significant part of my recovery.

Speaking of walks with friends, I must tell you about my friend Anne, who was a survivor of breast cancer. I just adore Anne. We became friends while riding the ferry to work together over the years. Anne was a real trouper and became one of my few cancer-survivor confidants (since I still wasn't involved in a support group). I felt comfortable with her, free to talk about my thoughts and feelings, about my treatment, and generally about what the hell was going on with all this cancer business. As it turns out, Anne reacted much like I had when she was diagnosed. She really didn't have time to have cancer. She had two small children at the time, and she never considered that anything would happen other than she would have her chemo treatment and be done with it. That was more than ten years ago. She was inspiring, and confirmed that I was on the right track to getting my life back.

One day we were walking around the little town where we live, enjoying the beautiful bay view, and talking about chemo treatment, when suddenly Anne said, "And why do they call it a 'treatment' anyway? Like you're at the spa or something!"

I laughed till I almost wet my pants. She was hilarious, and absolutely right. What else could they call it? Certainly not what it was. There is nothing at all spa-like about intravenous chemotherapy. I don't want to relive all those awful moments by retelling them here, so you'll just have to trust me; it's no picnic.

Right there and then, Anne and I made a pact that as soon as I was done with all my treatments, she and I would go to a real spa and have real "treatments." It was a beautiful fall day when we finally kept our promise and spent several deliciously decadent hours spoiling ourselves with massages and facials in the wine country to the north. What a treat! It was such a fun thing to anticipate at the time we were planning it—just when I needed *something* to look forward to—and it was such a joy to share some good times with a good friend. These are the moments that make up our lives, and I was committed to making more and more of them with each day I had left.

Persevering

SUMMER 2011

The first round of chemotherapy was less scary than the second. The first time you really have no idea what to expect. It's all a mystery, and you learn as you go. But once you've placed your hand on the stove, you know damn well you don't want to do it again. My second time was like that, as were the third and fourth and all the rest. I dreaded each and every one of the six visits to the cancer center, but I knew they had to be done.

One way I acknowledged the neurosis that came with the whole mess was to share it. Nice, I know—sharing neurosis. That's easier said than done, particularly if you're a private person who isn't accustomed to telling others the intimate details about your life. But here again, cancer provided a path that allowed me to grow closer to those who meant the most to me.

------------------------------ ------------------------------

June 16, 2011: Kvetching

Well, tomorrow is the big day. Again. Chemo round two will commence at 0900 hours. For the Penguin Ice Cap Team, however, the day will begin at the crack of dawn as we load up the coolers with dry ice, pack the caps, and head for the infusion center. I can hardly wait for the steroids, anti-nausea drugs, Benadryl, pain meds, and the like—and of course the flaming blow torches and bazookas to kill some more cancer cells. I'll be a walking pharmacy by nightfall. And of course I'll be wearing subzero Penguin Caps on my head for eight hours. So, people, before you start complaining about YOUR day tomorrow, just think of me, will ya? I guarantee that whatever you're doing it will be more fun than I'll be having.

I figured that before I throw myself on the floor and start sobbing (okay, maybe that's a bit too dramatic), I would try and think of some good things about chemotherapy. Here are a few:

Ten Good Things about Chemotherapy

- Lying around reading magazines, guilt free
- Saving time in the shower by not washing my hair
- Avoiding the Atkins diet program
- Getting to know my acupuncturist really, really well
- Learning fifty new recipes for protein smoothies
- Finding out exactly how many vitamins I can swallow at one time
- Enjoying a deeper appreciation for what "feeling great" truly means
- Walking around the block slowly enough that even my little Zorro can keep up with me
- Wearing my size 4 jeans again
- Not having to make up an excuse for not being at the office

Humor, once again, came to the rescue. That, and the fact that those crazy ice caps were actually working. Not a stranger anywhere had any idea that I was a cancer patient. The Huff was amazed. Without those caps, I would have been totally bald within a few days of my first treatment, but by the end of my second treatment I still had a full head of hair.

July 26, 2011: Capelli Update

Everyone says, "You don't even look like you're in cancer treatment. No one would ever know."

Yeah, baby. That's the idea.

The mantle of "survivor" slowly appeared as I put one foot in front of the other and plodded down the path before me. Cancer provides you with an opportunity to see exactly what you are made of, exactly who you are. It is an out-and-out battle to the death. Some of us, sometimes, get the upper hand. I was determined to do my very best and see how far I could push back the attacking troops. I was determined to survive.

Things I Have Survived

- High school.
- College.
- A cross-country move with only $80.
- Four multiday marathon bike rides, two with brown recluse spiders in my tent, two in torrential rain, and one with headwinds exceeding twenty-five miles per hour and hail. I rode every mile.

Floating over Albuquerque

- One hot-air balloon ride.
- Three years in law school. In godforsaken Lubbock, Texas. I shall never go to that place again. Never.
- Two bar exams.
- Seven years at a New York law firm.
- The loss of two dear and special furry companions, one of whom shared over seventeen of my most formative years.
- The death of both my parents, my dearest aunt, and my brother in every sense, Mike. Their wisdom continues to guide me, even today.
- One broken marriage.
- Two broken legs.

I will survive this too. Yes, I will.

Contemplating. That happened a lot as well. It may have been due in large part to having the time to contemplate, which few of us do, or to taking the time, which rarely seems an option in our rush-around world. But when you're in the midst of cancer treatment and are forcibly slowed to a crawl, there is time to think about the things that matter. In fact, you realize, truly realize, what *does* matter. It's no longer an abstract principle. It's very real. The fact of your own mortality and limited number of days left on the planet come into sharp focus.

Taking care of myself was job one. It had to be. There are so many things that tax your body while you go through cancer treatment that you have to remain vigilant about your own self-care. One of the things I made sure to do was take care of my mind as well as my body; that meant doing the things I loved with those most dear to me. Going to see one of my favorite musicians in concert, for example, was a good way to stay focused on the present and not dwell on dreading the future. Day trips, adventures, trying new things—these were all ways I employed to stay present and focused on getting well.

But then came the drug shortage. More than halfway through my chemo treatments, I found out the cancer center was out of one of my critical drugs, Taxol. There's a reason certain protocols are described as the "gold standard," a phrase used repeatedly by doctors when they outlined the treatment for my specific type of ovarian cancer. Carboplatin and Taxol are the gold standard. The manufacturer of Taxol stopped making it, without warning. Apparently, there are no Food and Drug Administration standards requiring advance notice, so the hospitals and physicians were left scrambling.

The alternative drug, Taxotere, reportedly resulted in a "statistically insignificant" difference in outcomes than Taxol had. I guess one's understanding of "insignificant" depends on whether you were in the 4 percent of Taxol recipients who out-survived the Taxotere recipients. The Huff said it was very effective. It's not that I didn't believe him, but hey, when you're in the middle of treatment you don't have much time to shop around for something new. We called every hospital and doctor we could think of, and no one had any left. In fact, unbeknownst to me, I had received some of the last Taxol in the region.

I wondered, approaching treatment number five of six, whether all had been for naught. Having to settle for a "statistically insignificant" but lesser drug might result in my cancer returning—despite my best efforts to eradicate it. But with nothing to do but complain to the pharmaceutical gods (who don't listen anyway), I took the Taxotere.

Perhaps the biggest mistake I made during my treatment regime happened during round five. I opted for less Benadryl than usual because Taxotere supposedly caused less of an allergic reaction than Taxol. What I didn't realize was that the intravenous Benadryl had made the subzero Penguin Caps tolerable.

Uh oh. Big mistake.

The hair-freezing adventure that day was practically unbearable. But there I was, committed to the process and blessed with hair with only two rounds of chemo left. I couldn't give up. Instead, I sucked it up and withstood the pain and migraine-like headaches for some nine hours that day.

As I have mentioned more than once already, one learns a lot about oneself in the battle against cancer. You learn what you are afraid of, you learn what you want, and you learn what you can endure. It seems to me that humans are a resilient lot with a zest for living. That natural instinct, bolstered by the love and encouragement of friends and family, go a long way to support the cancer patient's decision-making process and mind-set. We carry on because of it.

Undoubtedly, there are many patients far more ill than I was who succumb to barbaric treatment protocols with the hope that the cancer will be defeated. It's in the trying, after all. You don't know for sure what will work until you give it a go. My dear friend Mike fought bone-marrow cancer that way, all the way to the end. But at some point you call it a day. When the spirit and body are simply exhausted from the battle, they give in. We give up and allow ourselves to move on with our journeys. Each human being suffering with a terminal illness has that moment, and it is as individual as each person on

Earth. But until that moment comes, we fight. And the level of fight, too, is individual to each person. You really don't know what you have in you until the gauntlet is thrown down and you are faced with the challenge head on.

I suffered on with the caps and the drugs, and declared myself the victor over cancer that day after the sun had finally set.

Good News,
Annoying News

AUGUST 2011

DESPITE MY GOOD INTENTIONS, AND AS HARD AS I TRIED, THERE WERE the inevitable pitfalls and downfalls and the commensurate whining that accompanied them. Hey, I'm only human.

August 29, 2011: Good News/Annoying News

Good News: I weigh 131.5. Almost back to my welterweight. Just had fried chicken sandwich, fries, and milkshake at McD's. I note for the record that the milkshake likely contained no actual dairy product. Nor did the sandwich contain any real meat. Anyway, my white count is over 10,000 and enough to keep me from catching anything. Hopefully.

Annoying News: I have very few red blood cells. Very few, as I am almost ten points below normal. I have two choices: a blood transfusion (Ick! Someone else's blood?) or a Procrit injection. I opted for the latter with the hope that it will improve my cycling performance (wink, wink). At minimum, it should improve my ability to walk up my staircase.

Meanwhile, it's been a helluva week and an eventful night. I woke early in the wee hours with the equivalent of a severe charley horse across the middle of my back—shoulder blade to shoulder blade. Then, when I finally sat up on the side of the bed thinking I would try and lie on the floor and stretch out the pain, I passed out.

I came to with a giant bump on my forehead, a banged and scratched shoulder, and a bleeding gash on my arm. I must have hit the nightstand and God knows what else.

The Huff says anemia is causing it, and I shouldn't be out riding my bicycle alone. He did not forbid dance class, but if this past Saturday is any indication, I don't have the ability to really dance anyway. Turns out you really need red blood cells to do much of anything.

I am now officially pissed at this f%^&*ing cancer and its barbaric treatment. In spite of my cheery and optimistic outlook, and of course the positive results that the drugs have actually killed the active cancer, it is brutal. The bounce back from the treatments is taking longer and longer, and it will be months before my body starts feeling normal again. Yet three weeks from now I expect to be done forever with this bloody hell and pray that I can move on with a healthy life and forget the whole nightmare ever happened. I am sick, sick, sick of it.

Whining, party of one, your table is ready.

Most daily traumas in our lives pass, don't they? What seems so incredibly important or insurmountable on one day often fades into a distant memory the next.

Someone once said that worrying is a total waste of time. I'd have to agree. The analogy I heard involved the loss of a hundred-dollar bill. You can lament it, you can curse yourself for it, and you can berate your hectic schedule, the world's distractions, or your own stupidity. But given all the time you spend fretting about the what-ifs and ways to get that hundred dollars back, would it be worth paying that money to someone to return your peace of mind?

The more time I spend worrying, the more time I waste when I could be living. Worrying doesn't get us anywhere. It doesn't work. It doesn't help. It has no effect whatsoever other than to create anxiety. I followed the Huff's instructions and stopped worrying, and instead, kept taking one step at a time toward the end of the summer's long tunnel.

The Knockout Round

Finally, the day had come. After eighteen weeks and six rounds of chemo, it was almost over. Done. *Finito.* I could hardly wait. I spent the day before at the office doing blessedly mundane things. But I was more than ready for the final round and was looking forward to being on the mend for the last time.

Unfortunately, the last day did not go smoothly. By that point I was woefully short on veins, and the ones that were left were taking it pretty hard. My IV had to be pulled and reinserted several times, much to my everlasting dismay, because the veins were bubbling up. My arms ached and burned from the drugs, and my head ached from the caps. At one point I actually hid in the bathroom, head in hands, crying uncontrollably from the stress of the entire fiasco. It was many hours before I got out of there, making it the longest, worst day of them all. It lasted more than nine hours.

But then it was finally over. And just like that, an entire summer of laser-like focus on red cell counts, white cell counts, CA-125 test results, and killing cancer cells was finished. There was nothing left to do now but rest. Rest and wait.

Across the Great Divide

SEPTEMBER 2011

September 16, 2011: Across the Great Divide

At long last. The first week following the last cycle of drugs is over. I am eternally grateful to my best friend, Erika, for showing up with her ropes and gear to drag me across the abyss and keep me from falling in. The chemo has left me greatly dehydrated and still anemic, and without taste buds, but I am on my way back toward the surface of life where fresh air and bright sunlight await. May it all become a distant memory, and quickly.

IT GOES WITHOUT SAYING THAT SIX ROUNDS OF CHEMOTHERAPY REALLY do a number on your body. It would be a long time before my taste buds returned to anything like normal, which meant that I was saving a ton of money on grocery bills. Okay, so there was *that* upside, at least. But—like preparing for a big wedding, only to have it over in the blink of an eye—I was left without a daily target. No goal to meet. There was nothing else to do. Now I just needed to heal and recover.

It was then, in the aftermath of battle, when my mind actually began to grasp the immenseness of what I had been through and what it would mean in my life. The "blessings" of cancer began to reveal themselves more clearly.

Without realizing it, my running blog dialogue and musings with friends and family morphed into something deeper and more intimate. It was the awakening of newness and openness to everyone and everything around me, and the willingness to share my observations with those I cared about most deeply. In many ways, it was the opposite of the private life I had once valued. Having cancer had left me feeling exposed as a human being. And it was that exposure that drew my friends closer around; they were protective. But they also recognized—we all did— how precious our days and time together were.

I could no longer hide behind a profession or a relationship or the busyness of a schedule. Now I saw all too well the second hands ticking around the clock of life. Tick tock—each and every movement significant. The lessons came frequently and at random, and I welcomed them all.

September 23, 2011: "Consider Yourself Cured"

These were the Huff's words at our last appointment this week. I am elated, and still in a bit of shock.

This photo is proof that those damn Penguin Caps worked. Taken just days before my final treatment—I had hair after five rounds of chemotherapy. Unbelievable. Though I am grateful to their inventor, I shipped them back the very next day after my sixth and last treatment, as I just could not abide them taking up space in my freezer for one more minute!

I will close for now with an excerpt from one of my private journal entries during this little experience:

Journal Entry of July 16, 2011

Though I desperately want to erase this entire piece of my life once it has passed, I will hold deeply in my heart the love and support I have felt from my friends. It has been incredible. On those days when I can barely raise my head from the pillow, I am buoyed by an atmosphere of love and hope and energy and light and good wishes funneling to me through the cosmos directly to my heart. I am lifted. It is those relationships for which I am now more connected to this planet than the beyond. It is for them that I exist. What in the world I can ever give back to them I do not know, but I am joyful and grateful for having them all in my life. The hugs, the walks, the meals, the laughs, the phone calls, the tears, the everything I needed and when I needed it is what is bringing me through this nightmare day after day. I will look back and forget the cancer and the chemo treatments and my freezing scalp and bony body and lashless eyelids, but I will remember the connections I have on this planet and their significance in my life. I will never forget, and hope only that they will each call upon me in their time of need.

So get out there and live life to its fullest (whatever that means); you could be hit by a bus tomorrow. Or not.

Live as if each day were your last, but don't quit your
job lest you are wrong and end up living in a box under
a bridge. It is a delicate balance, these theories. Yet the
joy of a walk with a friend, a warm hand on your back,
or a meal provided by loving hearts is the essence of
what it means to be alive here. See the sky. No, really
look at it. Watch, really watch, a hummingbird for a few
minutes. Feel the tiny, little heartbeat of a five-pound
Chihuahua and look deeply into his eyes to see how
much he loves you, because now you know what love
really is. That connection. That silver-like thread that
grows and shines between you and the meaningful
others in your life. Our time here really is too short,
and that isn't just a catchphrase anymore. Whatever
"life" means to you, live it. Do not wait. Love. Love big
and openly and warmly and with great gusto. Don't
worry about dying without having made your mark,
whatever that mark may be. Most of us aren't Albert
Einstein, Gertrude Stein, or Rembrandt (or for that
matter a Kennedy or English royalty). They all made
their marks in their own way or for their own reasons.
Your mark may be nothing more than a clean diaper
for your baby, a hug for a friend who is going through
a rough time, or picking up a piece of paper from the
waterfront before it blows into our beautiful bay. Your
mark is everywhere. As Oprah has said, "Live your best
life." Well duh, right? But I get it now. Your best life
is whatever it is at the moment. Be happy, and make
others happy when you can. See what is around you
with new eyes. And above all, stop worrying. You have
control over so very little—why spend an ounce of time
worrying about it? Take that trip to Africa if you want
to; the bills will either get paid or they won't, and if
they don't, then at least you'll be in a frame of mind to

approach living in a box under a bridge as a whole new adventure.

Now, back to my normal life. I wish each and every one of you the very best and send all my love—

THE MOCKSTER

I finally began recuperating and stopped going to the office at all so that I could rest and recover. It was a very special time, but it was also the beginning of a new reality for me. Evidence of the new me manifested while I was recuperating at Erika's house the first few days after my final treatment.

I had tried throughout to keep up with work to some extent, at least enough to know what was going on and to provide clients with service where I was able. Toward that end, I participated in a conference call the morning before my last treatment, during which my client representative of several years handed off the case to someone new at the company. Lasting over an hour, the tedious call finally ended with the new chief-in-charge rubbing me the wrong way. Before the day was over, the new guy had sent me eighteen—count 'em, eighteen—e-mails that were "pressing," "urgent," or in which I was mandated to "make this a priority." It was a Thursday. I responded with a brief note acknowledging that I had received the multiple messages and that I would get back to him on Monday.

Monday morning found me still in pajamas and sitting at Erika's dining room table with my laptop. After spending about four hours diligently trying to respond to the various requests, I received yet another e-mail from the client rep. Instead of thanks, what I got was a terse response demanding even more. That was followed by a voice-mail message that resulted in an abdominal clenching of sorts. It was a feeling I knew all too well because it was bred in the fertile ground of client demands, endless time pressures, and twenty-four-hour availability.

I had lived with the stress and pressure of litigation for decades, but in the recent months I had become so attuned to my own body and its needs that the clenching was a discernible departure from what I wanted to cultivate: peace, rest, calmness. And so, for the first time in my professional career, I fired a client. It was a breakthrough moment for me that changed my trajectory. I no longer cared about client service in the typical way we've all become so accustomed to; that is, the client says, "Jump," and we say, "How high?" We endure abuse and disrespect and unbelievable demands that make us wonder if we're working for or *against* them. I was no longer willing to compromise my health for work. Quite possibly, it was the first time I realized I had been doing exactly that all along: waiting for the break that never came; pining for the vacation in the far-too-distant future; toiling day after day, absent any awareness of what the stress was doing to my body.

But now I knew. And I would not go back to where I had been.

No PETs

THE ONLY THING REMAINING WAS A FINAL PET SCAN TO COMPARE MY original results to my postchemo results. For the record, PET scans are no fun. At least not for me.

You show up and wait around for a while, and then they take you to a room and stick an IV in your hand or wrist through which they administer a radioactive isotope. There is only a small window of time to administer the isotope because of its limited shelf life, so the technician is always in a hurry. And you already know how I feel about needles. The creepy part is that they then leave you in a room by yourself as you stew in your own radioactivity. Once you've "cooled" (about an hour later), they then take you to the scanning room, where they run you back and forth through a giant donut hole a few times, with your arms stretched over your head. Nice.

I recall all too well my first PET scan experience. Back then—which seems like an eternity ago—I did my best to keep my chin up and just motor through so I could figure out what kind of cancer I had. But the moment they had left me alone in the room, I lost it. The darkness enveloped me, crowding out everything in my life beyond my cancer diagnosis. I had cancer. I was going to die. It was all so real then—or at least as real as I made it.

And now, a full cycle of chemo later, I was back at the imaging center. Doing the same thing. More jubilant than before, but equally as apprehensive about the needle-poking and the results. I was right on the first count.

November 4, 2011: In the Darkness

Unfortunately the procedure wasn't smooth sailing, as my veins have become tissue-thin from the chemo, and it took the technician three tries to get the radioactive isotope administered. Finally, once done, I sit alone in the darkness and ponder the long journey—from my first terrifying visit to this place in March until today. So much has changed. Most notably, today I am cancer-free, and this final scan will prove it. As I await my scan—radioactive, and listening to k. d. lang—I am grateful for the gift that is my life and my mother's spirit and encouragement to keep on keepin' on, despite life's travails.

There was another noticeable difference during the second PET go-round. Andrea was gone.

This shouldn't come as a surprise to any who have trod the cancer path before. It's a tough journey and not for the faint of heart. It is especially difficult on friends and family, and on girlfriends who probably never counted on having to deal with someone else's health crisis in the early months of carefree dating.

We had met online, and her Mensa-level intellect coupled with a gregarious sense of humor was irresistibly engaging. She was an engineer by profession, but her work history included an unexpected stint as a nanny to twin girls who continued to worship her even as they fled the nest to college and beyond. A Libra, she was incredibly sensitive and genuinely interested in taking care of others. Everyone who met her liked her, and we got along well despite the fact that our interests were utterly dissimilar. I was very much into fitness, an athlete and avid cyclist. She was more interested in intellectual pursuits and culinary delights. We could never play a board game together, for example, because—well, she was much smarter than I was, and I would get too stressed out because I had to think too much to play. I did that enough at work, day in and day out, and my competitive nature just wouldn't allow me to relax and have fun with it.

Although we cared very much for each other and shared a mutual admiration and respect, it was probably clear to both of us from the onset that we inevitably would go our separate ways. Ours was not a togetherness meant to last, with interests far too varied and which took us down far too different paths for any lifelong journey to be expected. As I realized while we were still together, sometimes the universe brings along someone in your life for a special purpose or reason. Andrea was just such a person. She provided friendship, caring, and support in immeasurable ways when I so desperately needed them. I am forever grateful to her as a result, and especially for heading up the Penguin Cap team.

Speaking of those crazy caps, they worked, all right. I had hair. I posted an "after" picture on the blog to prove it.

November 15, 2011: Postscript

And for the record, here's my hair after eighteen weeks of chemo (Carboplatin and Taxol—six treatments). Cheers to the Penguin Cap captain, Andrea, and her co-captain, Erika. Thank you.

One thing I hadn't contemplated, which came as a pleasant surprise, was how it would all end.

The day after the last treatment, I packed up those Penguin Caps and shipped them back to the company. It was my own monumental salute to the fact that it was all over. When I got out of bed the next day and looked in the mirror, I saw myself as I had always been, not as a cancer survivor who would have to wait a year or more for her hair to grow back. It was like hitting the reset button on my life, and I was fully ready to get back to it, hair and all. Externally, it was almost as if nothing had ever happened.

After my second PET scan, with results imminent, I hosted a celebration of life, inviting all those who had stepped up to provide me with care, nurture, support, and comfort during that long summer. I called it a joie de vivre (joy of life) party. It was a lovely opportunity to give thanks to those who had provided more than they knew, at a time when their help was so desperately needed—whether it was a ride to the doctor's office, a smoothie, carrying bags of dry ice, or visiting with flowers in hand. They were each a treasure that I counted among the pearls of wonder in my life. I toasted them individually, then shared something more personal.

"Back in July I wrote something in my private journal," I began. "I read it last night and it made me smile again, so with tongue-in-cheek I'd like to share it with you." Then, I read this entry:

> I've been thinking recently of what my good friend Patrick might say at my memorial service, should I have one prematurely. I hope it is this: "Jan convinced us all that she wasn't going to die. And we believed her. And even now she is probably as astonished as we are that she was wrong." I hope people chuckle at this. I hope they all know how incredibly certain I was—and am, even typing this today—that cancer isn't my death knell. It's been merely an inconvenience. A big one, mind you, but an inconvenience nonetheless. I intend to make it only a memory and a fading one at that.

Pausing, I added, "I have heard people refer to me as brave, but there's nothing brave about fighting cancer. Seems to me it's braver to forego the treatment and die, which medical experts will tell you is a certainty. I didn't do anything more than anyone else would have done in this circumstance—I made the choice to live."

A few days later I received the results of my second PET scan.

November 9, 2011: Joie de Vivre ...

I have just received word from the Huff that both my CT and PET scans are normal. Although I've had a positive attitude, I cannot express to you my deepest, most visceral and utter relief that this journey is over. I cried. The unleashing of held anxiety over these many months and months, the things I have learned, the pain endured, and the love I have felt. It is all too much sometimes …

2011 will now fade away for me as a bittersweet memory of a year that I hope and pray never to repeat. Ever. But I will cherish my deep connections with those who have carried me along this path. From the very core of my soul, I thank each one of you.

And now, let us celebrate together the Joy of Life. Onward!

Much love, Jan

The Big Surprise

NOVEMBER 2011

THE SUN BEGAN TO SHINE BRIGHTER ON MY NEW LIFE. IT WAS THEN, at the newly single stage of my more-enlightened eyebrowlessness that I miraculously happened upon that one special someone I had been waiting for all my life, as the song goes.

After weeks of being off the bicycle due to the unfortunate absence of red blood cells, I finally climbed back on board to join some friends for a leisurely ride near my home. It was on this ride, with a handkerchief wrapped around my thin ponytail, "doo rag" style, that I met Carole.

As I later recounted the story many times, I did a double take. She was strikingly beautiful in her black-and-red racing kit, on her black-and-red racing bike, and she was predictably fast. It was simply not possible, I thought. Here was this sublime woman on this improbable ride where no one ever showed up on more than a hybrid bicycle of one sort or another and with furry scarves wrapped around their handlebars in case of inclement weather. Carole was definitely out of place, and yet in the perfect place all at the same time.

It was love at first sight, for me anyway.

We ended up on several group rides together before I got up the nerve to ask her out on a date; my request was initially rejected. But try, try again, my mother used to say. And so I persisted.

While trying to figure out how to get her attention away from the bicycle, it occurred to me that I now had a set of problems I had not previously considered. I was a cancer survivor. How many people would willingly date someone recovering from ovarian cancer? Who would walk willingly into that kind of situation? Spending the rest of my life alone was not what I had in mind, but that prospect suddenly became very real for me. I could not imagine the shoe on the other foot, i.e., knowingly and willingly becoming involved with someone on the edge of cancer treatment with an unknown, likely short, future. That realization may have been the first time since the diagnosis that I felt stymied, and truly sad.

It was hard to figure out just what to do, but there was no question that a truthful disclosure would be forthcoming. The sooner the better.

Ultimately we did go to dinner, and the rest is history. But the important part of the history is that on our second date, I told her about my health issues. I worked hard to hold back the tears while I explained that I would understand if she chose to move on with her life. We could simply continue to be friends and ride our bikes together sometimes. It was painful.

And then came the surprise …

Carole took my hand, looked into my eyes, and said she wouldn't trade that moment for anything in the world. Cancer didn't scare her, and she wasn't willing to miss the opportunity of sharing a life of happiness with someone out of fear. She was on board. We next saw each other on Thanksgiving Day, when we met for breakfast, and she greeted me with a dozen rainbow-colored roses.

I frequently wonder what she really thinks about all this. We have matter-of-fact discussions now and then about my possible early demise. She disagrees with me, projecting a long life together into our eighties and beyond. I, on the other hand, am determined to retire sooner rather than later, in case I miss the "good years" working and saving for my old age—an old age I may never see. But Carole is a smart woman. While hope for a targeted cure springs eternal, she also comes from a medical and nursing background and knows, probably better than anyone, what this deal is all about. Nonetheless, she chose me, with my cancer. And that makes her the bravest and most courageous person I know.

Back in the Game

JANUARY 2012

I RETURNED TO WORK FULL-TIME IN JANUARY. WOW. WHAT A TRIP. IT was odd because, in a way, it was like I had never been away. The plants in my office had survived (thanks to one of the firm's staff members with a green thumb). Papers were still piled on my desk in neat stacks. The chairs sat just so, waiting for the next visitor to discuss the nuances of a case or the weather. All was the same as when I had left, including the long list of cases, to-do lists, and status updates I had prepared the spring before. It felt very, very odd.

But it wasn't too long before I realized two things. One, I had more free time than I was accustomed to having. Most of my cases had been resolved or reassigned in my absence. The things I should have been doing for the coming year were no longer on my plate. I basically had to start all over. But the second thing was even more surprising: I didn't have the heart to be there anymore. None of it seemed important enough.

I'd sometimes just sit and gaze out the window at the beauty of San Francisco Bay. And rather than focus on revising a legal brief or trying to do some business development, I'd think about how my life was ticking away day by day. How much better my time would be spent hearing about my friends' lives over lunch, about their joys, and their challenges; riding my bike with my newfound love; taking pictures of flowers; walking little Zorro; or just looking up at the sun and marveling at the immense ahhhhh-ness of it all. Instead I found myself back at my desk and unable to get my head in the game.

It's not that I didn't want to work. I did. I always had. My parents had instilled a strong work ethic in me, but my head was elsewhere.

One of the unexpected side effects of surviving cancer was apathy. Being an attorney was best suited to my skill set, but after I returned to work, apathy set in. Everything that once seemed so important now seemed meaningless. Sitting in partner meetings listening to people gripe about money, for instance. Meaningless. Enduring conference call after conference call battling over discovery matters (i.e., whether one party in a lawsuit will show evidence to the other party). Meaningless. Enduring asshole lawyers and clients who think they own the world, are inexorably rude, and who carry around so much anger in their own utterly miserable lives they feel compelled to spread it around to others. These people were no longer worth my time. During each one of these conversations I would think to myself, *I don't have time for this. I am literally wasting my precious life sitting here listening to you right now.*

Though it sounds presumptuous, I finally understood what was happening on this planet.

Much of our everyday lives can be described as a mere farce. Why? Because money doesn't matter. Politics don't matter. Gas prices do not matter. The only things that matter are love and our connection to other people. Spending time with the spiritual beings that give real meaning to our existence is what matters. The toys, the marketing, the advertising, the investments, the money—none of that matters. You most assuredly cannot take it with you, and fighting and clawing for it, rather than actually living, is like burying your soul in a vast wasteland.

My apathy lingered for almost an entire year, and the residual feeling remained. It resulted in the most unproductive year of my professional life. Billable hours meant nothing any more. Yes, I was glad to be back at work, but my focus was no longer on the number of hours I could rack up in a week, originating business, or collecting the almighty dollar for the firm. Unfortunately, some of my partners had not yet become so enlightened, though most of them seemed remarkably understanding of my low productivity, at least on the surface. The miserable and greedy ones, on the other hand, didn't even pretend. Their disdain was readily apparent.

It was an odd place to be in, that place of indifference. It wasn't something I was accustomed to and had never been part of my genetic makeup.

A Capricorn, I generally set goals and worked diligently to achieve each one. I was organized and efficient, a linear thinker. But my mooring had come loose, and I could not get a firm grasp on what I should be doing. I flailed here and there, wondering if I were better suited to work for a nonprofit defending helpless animals, or if I should devote myself to the cause of gay and lesbian equality. But those courses, while admirable, don't pay the bills. I had long been my own provider, with no one to rely on for support if I chose to take a sabbatical to figure out what to do with my life. I always envied those who enjoyed that luxury.

I met with an investment broker to talk about my "life plan." My plan, sort of, looked like this: I was interested in buying a house with Carole. I was pretty dissatisfied with my current but well-paying profession. Oh, and I just wanted to stop working. At the tender age of fifty-two.

Stop working?

Since age seventeen, when I first began my adult employed life, I had never once considered that prospect. The word "retirement" was not in my glossary. Yet having had a taste of life that didn't include a workload, client demands, tight schedules, and deadlines, I now knew what *living* felt like. According to the broker, the good news was that I had money in the bank. The bad news was that if I jumped ship today I would only have enough to last for ten years. That's more than most people, and for that I was immensely grateful, but no one really wants to run out of money and have to live in downtown doorways at the age of sixty-two.

The more interesting discussion with the broker revolved around that little thing called an actuarial table. She had done an analysis of my financial condition based on my living to the ripe old age of ninety-two.

"My dear," I said, "I won't be living until the age of ninety-two."

Maybe I will, and maybe I won't. But there are probably few ovarian cancer survivors who give themselves the long odds of living to a ripe old age. The problem is, you just don't know how long you have. I started thinking that maybe the smartest thing to do would be quit my job and live the rest of my life doing things that have meaning. Volunteering. Helping. Changing the world for the better. But just in case I was wrong, I decided to continue marching in the work-a-day parade in case I lived to be eighty, thought it was hard reconciling those two distinct realities.

And So It Began, Again

SPRING 2012

The end of cancer treatment represented a new beginning. The lessons were being learned, and by some sort of natural process, they began to be shared. My blog posts continued to change from reports of my physical well-being to things more esoteric, more meaningful. I began to share what I was experiencing as I learned to live with my chronic illness, which was no longer the death knell that I had once believed it to be. Instead, my self-awareness and appreciation for living seeped out in everyday observations.

March 19, 2012: Reflections

Yesterday was one year to the day since my cancer diagnosis in 2011. I can hardly believe now that it ever happened or how very long ago that day feels.

I thought I would take a moment to reflect on what I have learned during the last twelve months and how that event has changed my life. One thing is certain, life really is shorter than the cliché would suggest.

I have learned that it's very difficult sometimes to take my lessons and apply them to daily life. There are so

Caribbean Morning

many pressures from job and society that they often obscure what's really important. I continue to struggle with this daily, especially since returning to work earlier this year. Work, as we all know, takes up a LOT of time (a nod here to my retired friends; good for you for having reached Nirvana).

Try though I might, it seems impossible to get my head around the fact that life can and should be lived with little regard for the work it takes to exist in the day-to-day world. When I do try to live with such little regard, the laundry piles up and the bills don't get paid. Too bad our societal structure isn't set up in a way that would allow for more free time, more reflection, more relaxation (again, at least not until you reach those golden years). And yet when I manage to worm my way out from under the ever-present feeling that something must get done, I revel now even more than before in simply being, appreciating so deeply the ability to freely do the things I love, and with such joy. My body has rebounded in a remarkable way, and each day I care for and nurture her as a thank-you for pulling me through. There is such joy in dancing in class with my friends and riding my bicycle—it all just feels so good. It's like grabbing a lung full of air after you've been under water. Walking down the street, I see people in such a different way now, wondering how they came to be on this path, on this planet, at this time. Wondering what lessons they are learning or have chosen to learn along the way. Everything looks different. We are all going about our day experiencing what we see, smell, taste, and touch in a way that can only be experienced here, on this planet.

Someday it will be different, when our spirits move on to the next place. But today—having looked at my life and the shortness of it in such a profound way—I am loving my bright, shiny spot here on Earth. It is a privilege and, in some regard, I guess, also a burden. But we are all in this together.

The chemo took a toll on my body; though I had started at a high level of fitness, my red blood cells needed to rebuild. I knew those things would work themselves out over time. Meanwhile, I was determined to get back out there, and keep on doing what I had done before. The more fit I was, the better and faster my body would recover. And with that, I got right back on my bike and rode. It was a challenge at first, but I kept at it. My success in riding just a little farther, and feeling a little better, was a small victory each time. I decided to set a goal for myself: to participate in the Northern California Livestrong event once more, but this time as a cancer survivor. I had no idea when I signed up how meaningful that experience would be, even though in the past

I'd seen so many other cancer survivors cross that finish line to claim their single yellow rose.

Nine months after my last round of chemo, with a red blood cell count still climbing out of the crapper, I rode my bicycle seventy miles and raised $2,500 in my first-time-as-a-survivor Livestrong ride. Not only did I ride it, I smoked it! With the help of Carole, in whose draft I rode most of the way, I finished the course in record time with an average speed of about twenty miles per hour. It was a remarkable experience and one I won't soon forget.

June 27, 2012: Incredible

Photo courtesy of Christopher Gage.

That is the only way I can describe my first Livestrong Challenge ride as a cancer survivor. I knew I was physically fit to do the miles, but never did I expect I would do it with such gusto (many thanks to Carole, "the Hammer"). Only three hours and forty-two minutes of riding time. But even more surprising was the level of emotion that came, which was wholly unexpected. On previous rides, it had never occurred to me that I would one day be a "survivor" who would ride down the special chute to the finish line to receive a yellow rose. But on Sunday, June 24, 2012, I did just that. Not only did I receive a single yellow rose, but my bestest friend Erika surprised me at the finish line … carrying an enormous bouquet of two dozen yellow roses.

Photo courtesy of Christopher Gage.

We shared a gigantic hug and wept tears of joy at the year behind us and at the success we shared in beating that effin' disease. (A special thank you here, again, to the Huff and Dr. Shen for saving my life, and to Andrea for saving my hair.) What an incredible difference a year makes, as it was just this time last year that I had nailed two chemos down with three more to go. Sheesh …

Photo courtesy of Christopher Gage.

Anyway, I think of all the people who were so inspirational at the Livestrong event, and I hope they keep on keepin' on and inspiring others. After all, isn't that what we're here for? I hope in some tiny, itsy-bitsy way, maybe I've inspired someone as well by not giving up, by taking back my life, and by getting on with it. The T-shirt slogan for Livestrong this year is "Pick a Fight." I did. And I won. And that feels great.

Life Before

REFLECTIONS

It's hard to think back now to what I was like before. I'm obviously the same person, but I am remarkably different.

Before my diagnosis, I was a garden-variety trial lawyer. I graduated law school more than two decades ago. Funny, it seems like just yesterday that I was toiling away in the library, reading case after case and taking exams. Twenty years, two states, and two bar exams later, I find myself in much-beloved California where I will spend the rest of my days. I fell in love with this place more than a decade ago, and I'm not exaggerating when I say I love it here. It fulfills me in ways that no geographic area ever has. As for the job, unlike many lawyers I know, I actually like my job; but it's different now.

Prediagnosis, I thoroughly enjoyed the puzzle-like way in which a legal case is put together—the evidence, the briefs, the court hearings. I enjoyed the jury trials too, so much of it theatrics, though of the academic variety. The problem solving was challenging, as was the unfortunate scheme that is the engine of most law firms: the billable hour. With plenty of work to be done, I racked up the hours by doing as much as possible, at least during those first few years. There was always the reward—the money, especially at my first job with a New York law firm; the money was practically addictive. Among its benefits were opportunities to pay off my student loans, buy my first house, and get a nice car. I figured if I were going to be in the rat race, at least I'd be smart about it. But as the years passed and I ventured west, finding a firm that was nowhere near the sweat shop that the New York firm had been, I relaxed into what some euphemistically call the "work/life balance," well, for a lawyer anyway.

I did what most everyone else does each day—got up, set off for work, went home. I stayed late at the office whenever necessary to get this or that accomplished, and had dinner with friends when I could fit them in the schedule. I'd walk my little dog when I got home, if I had time and it wasn't dark. And dinner was almost always a salad and some tasty treat from a cardboard box that I shoved in the microwave. Day in and day out, with the occasional vacation. That was my life. It was routine and comfortable, and I was generally happy with the way things were. My routine included bicycling, of course, as that has been part of my life longer than I've been a lawyer. My days were full.

Nobody's life is perfect, and mine was no exception. I'd survived a divorce, the death of both parents, a broken leg with partial paralysis from a skiing accident, and other of life's travails. When beaten down, I would get up again and keep going. My mother was one of those "pull yourself up by your bootstraps" kind of women. She had somehow managed to survive the loss of a young child, a miscarriage, and her own bout with cancer. She taught me well. I survived. I was blessed with many friends, community activities, and love. And I was over fifty, which I considered a very good thing. There's something interesting about fifty. It's an age where you no longer feel beholden to anyone or the need to prove anything to anybody. You generally know who you are, what you want, and where you're going. At least you think you do, until cancer slaps you upside the head.

The Road Ahead

OBSERVATIONS

MORNINGS ARE A FUNNY TIME. I'M NOT A MORNING PERSON, BUT I frequently get up early on a weekday to squeeze in a little bike ride before hopping on the ferry across the bay to work. Today, I'm still suffering from a bit of jet lag though, and my body is saying no to the moist, cool air outside my window. The high fog hangs over Sausalito like a chuppah at a Jewish wedding. Today I'll skip the ride because the future is on my mind, and I want to share my thinking. But with whom?

Trouble is, I don't actually know my thinking. Planning for the future is as difficult for me as baking a pineapple-upside-down cake. I'm no cook, never was. But I used to be pretty good at planning.

Non sequitur: my father urged payment of all debts; he never wanted to owe anybody anything. He was also a bit of a miser, having survived the Great Depression, and having wanted for shoes at various points in his life. I have generally followed his course and kept my debts low, but in recent years have spent money on things that I want but don't need, or that give me pleasure—traveling, a new convertible, or a new bicycle, for instance. I justified what my father would deem unnecessary expenditures as a reward for working so hard.

"The one you've got's still workin', ain't it?" he'd say with his southern drawl. "So long as it's workin' ..." Then his voice would trail off, no doubt lamenting the money I was wasting.

Despite my father's good teachings, I know that spending money now and then isn't a bad thing. Yet with each purchase, though there are few, I cringe a little inside as I hear his voice from beyond the grave, telling me I don't need whatever has caught my attention.

How does this relate to planning? Simple. Thus far, I've been the workaday professional. Work hard. Save for retirement. Spend little. Put money in the bank. Each day at the office was a chance to bill more hours, make more money, get in a higher compensation bracket.

But that's all changed. Now, I'm a model of indifference. I can't get excited about running into the street and beating the bushes for new clients. When a case settles and I'm left with free time on my hands, I relish the vacuum. Being on disability leave miraculously revealed exactly what I've been missing all these years: the freedom to enjoy living; the joy of having free time.

I've worked since I was seventeen, either in school or at a job or both. I've never had more downtime than the few weeks I took between the bar exam and starting my first job as an attorney. Since then, it's been the life of a trial lawyer. Now, I daydream about all the things I could be doing instead of sitting at my desk. But there is no time. I figured out that I spend about five waking hours out of twenty-four in my house. The morning hours are usually taken up by exercising, showering, and then rushing to catch the ferry to work; the evenings are consumed with walking the dog, making something to eat, and then the multitude of tasks on my to-do list— bills, laundry, answering e-mails. There is precious, precious little time for creativity, soul-searching, or writing.

And the phrase "little time" has taken on a whole new meaning for me; it is now "bonus time." It's the bonus time that I think about. How am I spending it? How should I be spending it? It's pretty clear that my time on this planet is limited, and I wonder what one thing I am supposed to be doing. If one believes, as I do, that we are all here for a purpose—to teach and to learn—then I wonder what my purpose is? I must meditate more on this and cozy up to my core self in order to hear that voice within that will tell me which doors to open and which to ignore.

Meanwhile, I am having difficulty making decisions to plan my life. Carole and I want to live together, but we both own homes (she's had hers for twenty-five years, and it's paid off, lucky her!). Should we sell them both, and buy a new home together? Is incurring that kind of debt at fifty-plus, as we both are, the smartest thing to do? Should we rent our places and buy a house using our retirement savings as a down payment? I just can't seem to come to a decision as I swing between the financial risks, the benefits, and my emotions. But as I said to Carole the other night over dinner, always at the back of my mind is knowing (or not knowing) how much longer I'll live. Of course, no one does. But that amorphous concept is front and center and very real in my life, and for good reason.

At the end of chemo, when I was practically gloating at having kicked cancer's ass down to a CA-125 score of only 8, I asked the Huff, "Why does ovarian cancer get such a bad rap, when it's completely treatable?" I was not expecting his answer.

"Because it comes back," he said. "It can come back. That's why we have to keep up with regular monitoring, so that we can watch it. And if it does return, we can treat it immediately."

My eyes welled with tears and I hung my head. "Really," I whispered, more matter-of-fact than questioning.

The Huff tried to reassure me that it doesn't always come back, and that there was nothing to indicate it would do so in my case. But the words hung in the air like a noose from a tree branch.

And that noose is always there. Having survived cancer once, I now know the harshness of the endeavor. Could I do it again? I would hope I would try, but I cannot promise, because a war is far easier waged the first time than again and again. That goes for most things, doesn't it?

I asked the Huff if I should be planning for retirement or if I should be making sure there were no more than ten dollars in the bank when I kicked the bucket. He urged a balance between the two, saying that planning for the future is not only appropriate, it's smart. He's right, I'm sure, but something deep within leaves me uncertain. My entire focus is on spending my life in a healthy and productive way, not on wasting any time, and having as much fun as possible. I want to see the things that are here to see, do the things that are here to do. Experience. Live. I don't want to spend my days crunching out billable hours, or worrying about not having enough of them.

After more than twenty years practicing law, I know I'm good at it. Organizing and problem solving are two of my best skills. But the profession itself no longer holds the attraction for me that it once did. Although I certainly enjoy the job security it provides, I'm just part of the 99 percent who are tied to their jobs for the insurance coverage. And given my medical history, I can hardly consider starting my own firm. Having cancer affects so many things that you'd never think about otherwise. Having good health insurance is just one of them. Thankfully, we have moved toward a model of national health care in this country; still, there are millions of Americans who are without medical coverage. I find that outrageous. I have insurance, and yet my medical expenses for my cancer treatment and recovery were tens of thousands of dollars out of my own pocket. It's a disgrace, and I cannot imagine being faced with such a disease and not having the ability to treat it.

In any event, I am trying to become reinspired in my chosen profession by attending networking events instead of having dinner with friends. That's a hard one. Yes, networking is important and that's what I should be doing, but I find myself more attracted to dinner with my friends so we can catch up on each other's lives. Nurturing my friendship with Erika, for example, seems like a better way to spend three hours rather than yammering away with people I will probably never see again.

In my humble view, the work/life balance theory is a fantasy. Sure, it's okay to take a vacation, or coach your kid's little league team, as long as when the end of the year comes you have billed your allotted share of hours and collected your pile of money to throw in the pot. With few exceptions, part-time attorneys typically become no-time attorneys. It's just not in the cards for this profession.

I read with some cynicism a draft of a strategic plan for my law firm. It's a wonderful work-in-progress, full of ideas, direction, and strategy. It actually uses the words "work/life balance" on three occasions, but only as filler or the title to a section heading. There's not one substantive word as to what work/life balance actually means. Rather, there are several indicators that each partner must either row the boat forward, and fast, or be thrown overboard. Like every other law firm, it's really all about the money. The mission statement says nothing about work/life balance, but does specifically say the firm's goal is to "work hard" (and provide excellent client service, of course). I suppose I have a "bye" during my first year back to work after a major health crisis. But I definitely didn't expect this level of inactivity, inattention, or lassitude. It surprises me.

What will I do now? I don't know. Finding something that is a passion and also pays the bills will be a challenge. If you're passionate about something for which there is no market—for example, reading Tolstoy or making trivets out of bottle caps—that will not put much money in the bank. But if you're a passionate gardener, you can probably turn that into a pretty decent living. I've been a lawyer for so long now—after almost starving as an artist in the early years—I don't know what else I should do with my life, or what else I *could* be doing.

I keep thinking that my love of animals should lead me to a nonprofit job where I could practice law in the animal legal defense realm. Yet it seems like all the worthwhile causes don't pay well. But isn't that the way it always is? Civil rights lawyers are doing justice in the world, and yet they get paid so little. Unless you're David Bois or Ted Olsen (the lawyers in California's Proposition 8 battle)—who have enough money in the bank to be able to spend time working for free—a pro bono docket isn't going to keep a roof over your head or food on the table. Like teachers, "do good" lawyers usually don't make much either.

Funny thing is, I wouldn't even be having this conversation with myself if I had not had cancer. I was on track to have a banner year—speaking engagements, new cases, the works. Then came the diagnosis. Everything changed. The brevity of life and the experience of free time have all led me to this point, and I am reluctant to go backward.

Fear Factor

MORE OBSERVATIONS

It's back there— the fear, that is— in the back of my mind. I got a book at the beginning of my treatment called *The Worry Solution* by Martin Rossman and Andrew Weil. It is a pretty good book that taught me how to handle the fear when it crept in and threatened to consume me. I learned how to divert my mind to something else when those unwelcome feelings flared. My therapist told me many times that the brain is a functioning organ like any other. From our earliest days on Earth, as human beings who lived off the land, searched for food, and hid from predators, the brain has alerted us when a threat, real or perceived, is nearby. When the fear starts to rear its head, I stop, take a deep breath, and remind myself that my brain is just trying to keep me safe from animals in the jungle.

One can appreciate the fact that, on any given day, our brain sends off multiple fear singles—alerts that prevent us from walking down a dark alley, stepping in front of a fast-moving car, or approaching an unfriendly looking dog on the sidewalk. Unfortunately, our brains are bombarded every day with fear messages. Fear of getting fat. Fear of looking bad. Fear of missing out on a mattress sale. The media and merchandisers have figured out that our brains respond to fear and will motivate us to act, usually by buying whatever they're selling so that the feared thing doesn't happen to us. The fear is always there, to protect us, more or less. But now my brain has a little extra stimulus—my ongoing battle with cancer. Perhaps if I'd bought those special vitamins or green juices Whole Foods hawks, I could have avoided all of this.

Fear creeps in at times when I'm not paying attention, catching me off guard and leaving me overwhelmed. Every couple of months I go to see the Huff and have a blood test. I diligently swab my arms with Lidocaine numbing cream, wrap them in gauze, and make my way into the city for one of my least favorite tasks. While I am usually pretty good about putting away thoughts of "what if," my brain wrestles me to the mat sometimes:

> What if it comes back? Today's blood test was four points higher than the last. What does it mean? What will it be next time? Should I never eat sugar again? Don't cancer cells feed on sugar? What about wine? Should I just stop enjoying wine altogether? And I need more sleep. If only I could get more sleep I would be able to keep control of what's going on inside my body.

I sometimes forget what great shape I was in when I was first diagnosed. Unfortunately, I know all too well that one can be terrifically physically fit and still have cancer. The fear sometimes drives me to do things that I wouldn't have done a year ago. I'm apathetic at work because I'd rather be doing something else. I fear I'll run out of time to see Australia or make new friends or do all the things I want to do with the love of my life. What if the cancer comes back? I realize I can't spend much time thinking about the "what-ifs" because it doesn't serve me in any positive way. Worrying about it will do absolutely nothing to prevent it. Instead, I try my damnedest to focus on the things I enjoy doing on this planet and just live in the present, which is really all I have.

The Wisdom

AUGUST TO SEPTEMBER 2012

One by one, cancer's teachings became clear. I began seeing people in a different way. A new way. The walk to work from the Ferry Building at the end of Market Street, for example, was an opportunity to experience that slice of humanity that is San Francisco: the tourists and street vendors, the skateboarders and bicyclists and techies with smart phones in hand. I'd pass countless homeless people or beggars on the street, and slowly I realized we were really all the same. But for a twist of fate, or a different gene combination, it could easily have been me lying on the sidewalk. Did any of them have cancer? Did they need treatment? How far were they from the end of their days? What about the woman in the dark coat and sensible walking shoes in a rush to God-knows-where. What was she dealing with in her life?

There was so much sameness about all of us, and yet we were all intensely different in so many ways. I was just one of the thousands and thousands of souls that make up the human race, surviving as we do on this big rock, scampering across the pavement among the tall buildings of the Financial District.

I have always loved the outdoors, especially the ocean. As though I was looking out an airplane window at a landscape dotted with little houses and cars, I now saw the earth in its grandest scale. I was reminded on a daily basis of my favorite Carl Sagan line about the universe being "an awful waste of space" if this rock is all there is. I *saw* things when I looked at them.

And I had questions, the type of questions that every human being asks himself or herself at one point or another: why *am* I here?

My blog became a way for me to share with others the thoughts and emotions and experiences that presented themselves to me. Something had changed me forever. The immediacy of life was clear, and I felt frustrated by our very limited time here on Earth. I struggled with my desire to experience it all while simultaneously hanging on to the carousel that we ride each day to support ourselves. Occasionally, well, frequently really, I stopped to take inventory and count my blessings.

August 15, 2012: Good Luck

My friend Joe says he misses my blog posts, but doesn't care so much about my blood test scores. He cares more about what I have to say about, well anything, I guess. He's a nice guy. Maybe too nice. So for Joe (and the rest of you), today I will report that my take on life is mostly about luck. Plain, old-fashioned luck. You can plan and work and struggle and try, but so much of where you end up is just about luck, isn't it?

Today I'm lucky that my CA-125 score went up only four points—to 14.4—instead of something astronomical, and that I'm keeping cancer at bay. Today, I'm lucky that I'm not starting chemo again. I'm lucky that I can walk around, instead of rolling around in a wheelchair. I'm lucky I can ride my bike. I'm lucky that I was born in the USA to two parents who loved and cared for me, and who were themselves lucky enough to provide me with a proper education. I'm lucky that I got into law school, and lucky to have a job doing something I enjoy. I'm lucky to have a nice place to live and transportation to get around. I'm very lucky to have a host of absolutely amazing friends, without whom my luck would have run out a long time ago. I'm lucky to have found true love.

Today, I am lucky to enjoy a life far removed from the despondency of Syria and the Middle East. I'm lucky to see the sun, and to be able to see at all. I'm lucky to have dreams and plans for the future.

Today I'm lucky to be alive.

Luck led me to Rome once again, almost one year to the day after the end of my cancer treatment. It was August 2012, and the end of summer vacations for all. The city was teeming with tourists of every variety, and the streets were packed. I'd not noticed so much graffiti during my earlier visits, but amid the chaos I was determined to find Laura's old apartment and take that much-anticipated photograph.

With Carole's help, I was able to locate the place using clues from the photograph and the map function on her smart phone. We made our way across the Tiber River Bridge to Trastevere. There we found the exact spot where Laura's postcard picture had been taken years earlier.

Carole crossed the street to duplicate the backdrop and take my picture standing in front of the steps of the small piazza. While she was maneuvering through the traffic trying to find just the perfect angle from across the street, my eyes swelled with tears, and I got the now-familiar choking feeling in my chest. I had made it! The moment I promised myself long ago, in the throes of just trying to stay alive, had arrived. I had returned to Rome and would send the picture to Laura as requested. I had survived, and survived well.

I shared that special moment with friends and family on my blog when I returned. Until that time, none of them knew about the postcard or my goal. Not even Laura.

September 19, 2012: Joie de Vivre, Italian Style

Just back from celebrating life in Italia. What a spectacular place it is, from the beautiful scenery to the delectable food to the warm and friendly people. Though it was unseasonably hot, I am proud to report I survived a weeklong bike trip through Tuscany, and in great shape. I also survived a second week of power shopping, wine tasting, and sightseeing. Once again I am reminded of all the beauty there is out in the world beyond the office … and to enjoy every minute of it. The time we

have left on this clod of dirt hurling through space is so
limited.

I took a special little sojourn while in Rome. My Italian
teacher, Laura, sent me a postcard last summer when I was
<u>not</u> on a European vacation. In it, she sent her good wishes
for my speedy recovery, and a challenge: Once my chemo
was over, she said, go to Rome and take a picture standing
in front of her old apartment, which was pictured on the
front of her card. Well, while in Rome, I did just that. Here's
the postcard she sent of her former flat, with the special
message on the back. I kept it on the mantel in my
bedroom for over a year as a reminder of my goal.

Photo courtesy of Laura Haber.

Now here I am
standing on the
corner holding her
postcard, on which
she writes, "non tutto
il male viene per
nuocere" (not all bad
comes to harm you).
Right she was.

That two-week trip with Carole was my miracle vacation—a second bike tour through Tuscany, self-guided to places I had never been, including the beautiful Chianti region and a small, charming town that is now my favorite: Castellina. I biked hard for five days in a row, climbing hill after Tuscan hill. I felt great. I was whole, healthy, and very, very happy spending time with the love of my life despite the unseasonable heat wave that had plowed its way across our vacation plans. We finished our trip in Rome at the very place I had seen innumerable times in Laura's picture.

Grateful didn't begin to cover it.

My days were bonus ones, and I vowed I would take none of them for granted. The metamorphosis was well underway.

September 28, 2012: Anais Nin

Yesterday's Bike Ride

Just read this quote from 1946. Thought I'd share …

The secret of a full life is to live and relate to others as if they might not be there tomorrow, as if you might not be there tomorrow … This thought has made me more and more attentive to all encounters, meetings, introductions, which might contain the seed of depth that might be carelessly overlooked.

This feeling has become a rarity, and rarer every
day now that we have reached a hastier and more
superficial rhythm, now that we believe we are in touch
with a greater amount of people, more people, more
countries. This is the illusion which might cheat us of
being in touch deeply with the one breathing next to us.
The dangerous time when mechanical voices, radios,
telephones, take the place of human intimacies, and the
concept of being in touch with millions brings a greater
and greater poverty in intimacy and human vision.—*The
Diary of Anaïs Nin*, vol. 4, 1944–47

Amen.

I had done a complete turnabout on how to live my life. Having
started with the Capricorn's desire to control everything, complete
every project, avert every potential negative happenstance—and failing
miserably—I had finally taken to heart the lessons that were being
forced upon me. One of the greatest was to stop wasting time fretting
over the past.

No matter how great, or how grave, the past is over and done. The
only possible good that can come of it is to learn from your mistakes
in order to avoid repeating them. Beyond that, the constant replay of a
missed opportunity, a denied promotion, a lover's betrayal, or the death
of a loved one is nothing more than an unhealthy and debilitating denial
of the life and joy that are right in front of you every day. Time is also
wasted on the "someday" fantasy of living in bigger houses, with more
money, better jobs, and smaller dress sizes.

Embrace this moment in your life. That's not to say that if the
way you are living isn't serving your best interests that you shouldn't
change it. On the contrary, if things are not as you want, and you
have the power to change them, then do. Nothing is stopping you but

you—unless you're only twelve; then maybe your parents will have a thing or two to say about it. But if you're old enough to be reading this book, then you're old enough to make decisions for yourself, and for your *best* self. Do this whether or not your decisions serve the needs of everyone around you. Let me remind you, as cancer reminded me: you're in this on your own. You came into this world alone, and you will leave it alone. It is up to you to be the best person you can be, and you can only do that if you find your own center around which your true self revolves. Unless you are truly happy with yourself, you cannot make anyone else happy.

Oddly enough, I found inspiration from an unsavory movie I saw once, starring Diane Lane. (She's a repetitive theme with me, I suppose, since one of my favorite films is *Under the Tuscan Sun*.) In this film, *Unfaithful*, she betrays her husband with some random gigolo she meets on the street. At their first meeting, he hands her a book and asks her to read a passage that today resounds deeply in my life. It is the words of Omar Khayyam: "Be happy for this moment. This moment is your life."

I saw those words written on a note card in an airport once, and I bought it because I was attracted to the charm of the notion it represented. Now, postenlightenment—as I sometimes refer to my postcancer days—I truly understood what the words mean. I found the card sometime during that summer of cancer treatment, and it made its way onto my entryway table, where it is a constant reminder of where my focus should be.

One thing I have learned to cope with is fear, which is a normal part of living for a cancer survivor. Well, probably for everyone, really. Everybody is afraid of one thing or another. Cancer survivors are afraid of the cancer coming back, facing another round of treatments, not finishing whatever we're supposed to be doing on this planet. Most of the time, though, we get up, go on with our day, and try not to think about it. But on those days when you can't help but think about it, it can be all-consuming. It doesn't matter what your "it" is. We've all been there.

My suggestion, learned firsthand, is this: Stop. Breathe. Just be. Know that everything will be as it is, but for now, only this moment matters. It's really all we have, after all. Don't fear the fear. It's part of what makes us human. Just let it go, and be where you are.

The Armstrong Saga

SEPTEMBER 2012

DURING MY BICYCLE TOUR IN ITALY, RED BLOOD CELLS FINALLY BACK and happily multiplying, I found myself relaxing over an early morning coffee and croissant atop the beautiful *poggio* known as Siena. It was there that I first heard the news of the Lance Armstrong scandal.

The US Anti-Doping Agency (USADA) released a report (there was never a trial) uncovering a so-called extreme doping operation within the US Postal Service cycling team. I was astonished, and upset. Having raised money for the Livestrong Foundation both before and after having survived cancer, I believed in its mission to support families and victims of the disease. And as an avid cyclist, and cancer survivor, I struggled to reconcile how someone like Lance could have done such a thing.

There were at least two separate camps on the issue, and some of my close friends were incredulous and openly challenged my position. I was a defender. How could I not be? Since then, of course, Lance has confessed his misdeeds to Oprah and others. Thus, it is with some trepidation that I share my long-ago blog post here.

❖

September 2012: Thank you, Lance

I awoke this morning to the news that the UCI (the international cycling organization) has taken away Lance Armstrong's seven Tour de France titles. Not surprising, given the hubbub of activity since USADA released its unchallenged evidence against him two weeks ago. Clever, I thought, that they would implicate the UCI itself by insinuating that UCI looked the other way for almost a decade. A brilliant tactic to ensure that UCI would do what the USADA itself could not—strip Lance of his tour wins.

I am troubled by this entire episode for so many reasons, but this morning I spent some time thinking about why this particular chapter really bothers me. It is my cancer talking, as I sometimes say, so forgive me for this.

Lance Armstrong has long been a hero to many cancer victims and survivors. It was not about the bike. It was about hope. The hope that your life could turn around and you could become normal once again. That every moment wouldn't be filled with the struggle against cancer, the battle to survive. It could go far beyond that. You could come back from the brink and succeed. Indeed, you could excel. It was that message of encouragement to so many that inspired Livestrong. It was about living, not dying.

I am troubled that someone like Travis Tygart at the USADA felt it was his personal mission to elevate himself into the limelight as the gotcha guy. Old Travis must feel supremely vindicated this morning to have seemingly destroyed an icon to so many. What he obviously doesn't understand is that in taking down a once-great American hero, he may have sucked the hope away from those who looked at Lance's achievements as a milestone they themselves could perhaps reach in their own individual lives.

My feelings on this are twofold. First, as one who survived six miserable rounds of chemotherapy myself, I cannot imagine that an athlete, even Lance, could bring himself to further poison his own body with doping. It just defies any logical resolution in my mind. I just cannot get my head around it.

Second, I look at the other aspect of all this. If, as the reports seem to indicate (and no, I haven't read all of the uncross-examined evidence yet), doping in the sport was so utterly rampant that everyone was doing it, then why single out Lance? If all his teammates and competitors were doing the same thing, then the playing field was level. If they were all jacked up on some drug or other, then why did he alone win the tour seven times in a row? Did he work harder than the others? Many past accounts have said yes; the man was a training machine. Does he just have better genetics than the other riders? Perhaps. I recall a long-ago documentary about how Lance was to bicycling what Michael Phelps was to swimming. He was just built to ride. Greater lung capacity. Greater VO2 max. So even assuming that the allegations are true, he still beat everybody else out there in one of the most grueling sporting events in the world today. And, drugs or no drugs, he came back from the brink of death to do so.

As disturbed as I am by all of this, I still believe in the power of hope and tenacity and courage and struggle and determination. I still believe in all the same things that Lance himself once believed in to get himself from the hospital bed to the podium. It is that hope upon which Livestrong was based. It is about living and living strong. It is about never giving up. It is about life, not death. It is about facing down one of the most deadly and terrifying threats there is and coming out victorious.

For bringing that fight to the fore, I thank Lance. For being the face of victory— not over other riders in the peloton, but over cancer—I thank him. Thank you, Lance.

Ignore It

SEPTEMBER 2012

A NEWSPAPER HEADLINE READ, "OVARIAN CANCER SCREENINGS ARE Not Effective." It was one of the first articles I'd read in well over a year about ovarian cancer, and then a bit tenuously. There were plenty of horror stories to go around, and all of them scared me. Ultimately, I decided that it did not serve me well to digest the articles and plethora of Internet information about ovarian cancer because it wasn't *my* story. I had my own plan. I had shunned the doctor who regaled me with statistics about low success rates. Instead, I favored the Huff, who had a view on life that mirrored my own.

"You've got it, let's take care of it, and meanwhile just go on living your life the way you have been. There's nothing stopping you," he'd say. And that's exactly what I did.

Go ahead, call it the ostrich effect. But it worked, for me anyway.

As I already mentioned, I was not into the support group thing. I also generally avoided all conversations about other people with cancer— most of which result in death, right? Time after time, if someone knew I had cancer they'd say, "My aunt died of breast cancer," or "My sister had it," or "We lost our dad to lung cancer last year …" It was an old and predictable refrain.

So why go there? Even today I avoid those conversations. There's enough uncertainty in all our lives as it is without piling on more uncertainty simply because you've had a cancer diagnosis.

During the treatment process I uncovered innumerable resources for this pandemic. And I mean innumerable. There's a whole world out there filled with cancer patients who have been successfully treated and are living out the rest of their lives in full and rewarding ways.

In many ways, cancer is just another illness like those treated every day in America's hospitals; you get your chemo or your surgery, and you go on. Sadly, though, the success stories don't garner many national headlines. I suppose if a full-blown cure is found, that might make the news. But for the tens of thousands of us who have received our treatment and are now back in the saddle, there's not much newsworthy about us. I guess that's understandable, but you'd think that sharing success stories instead of sad statistics more often would be more beneficial to people who are facing their own battles, wouldn't you?

"Say, just wanted you to know that we understand this is an awful situation right now, but you'll be fine." Those are the words you want to hear. Those are the words I did hear. And it was that hope and belief that kept me putting one foot in front of the other until I had made the passage from cancer patient to cancer survivor.

Listening Within

NOVEMBER 2012

SOMETHING HAPPENED ONE DAY THAT HAD NEVER HAPPENED TO ME before. I lost my little precious dog— as in, he disappeared.

He was fourteen years old, black, and weighed a hefty five pounds. He was practically deaf, without teeth, and had impaired vision. I was his sole guardian and had been his mommy all his life. Generally speaking, I spent lots of time asking "Where's Zorro?" just to keep him in my sight, lest some horrible malady befall him: A victim of cute-napping? Run over by a car? Hugged too hard by an eager child? You name it, this mommy worried about it. That day, though, was different. He was actually and suddenly gone; he wandered out of the yard while I was busy doing something else. *Gone.*

Denial set in. I kept looking inside the house, where I knew he wasn't, and around and around the yard, where I also knew he wasn't. I could tell. I could just feel his absence. Anyone who has ever lost a furry companion or a loved one knows exactly what I mean. The house is empty of their energy and their life. Their psyche is missing. It's palpable. That day was like that. I finally followed the trail through the only hole in the yard where he could have possibly escaped, which—to my horror—took me to a service road beside the highway and down a mercilessly long street to nowhere. I circled the house, and the block, asking everyone if they had seen a little black dog. Nothing.

After twenty minutes I was nearing a complete meltdown, then I retraced my steps again for the fourth time. I decided to follow the gap in the fence once more, willing myself to be that little guy. Where did he go? He's so small he could fit in a crack, hide behind a leaf. Anywhere. He could be anywhere. Panic set in.

Jogging down the sidewalk, I ran into several more people.

"Did you see a little black dog?" No. Nada. Nothing. I went to an apartment complex, where I ran into a nice woman who spoke no English. She called her daughter.

"Have you seen a little black dog?" I asked the young girl.

"No. Sorry," she answered, proud to use her new language.

I retraced steps to the sidewalk again, looking under every bush. Then suddenly I stopped. I took a deep breath, put my hands over my face, and cried, "Zorro, where are you? Please. Please tell me where you are."

And then, to myself I suddenly said out loud, *Stop, Jan. Feel for him. Feel where he is.* As I walked forward ten more steps, I knew I had gone too far. That unmistakable emptiness was there on the sidewalk; it was like walking into a dark room out of the sun. He wasn't ahead. I stopped dead in my tracks, turned around, and headed back.

I had taken no more than eight steps when a man came down the driveway of a second apartment complex, asking if I were looking for a little dog named Zorro.

"Yes," I exclaimed. "Yes, yes! Do you have him?"

"Yep. Safe and sound," he replied.

I finally exhaled. "Oh my God. Thank God!" I exclaimed.

The guy could not have been nicer. He led me back to his apartment at the end of a driveway I had not turned down. His two-year-old son had spied Zorro out the window, standing in the drive and staring blankly, and summoned his father. "Daddy. Dog. Daddy. Dog," he babbled, pointing outside.

The father told me that at first he was skeptical, thinking his son was simply confused since his own two dogs were inside the house. But to his surprise, when he looked out the window, there stood little Zorro. They took my little guy inside and the man's wife tried to comfort him. Needless to say, we were elated to see each other and I received the Zorro welcome that I had become accustomed to over the years: fervent tail wagging and relentless kisses on my nose. He was my best little buddy and friend, and I had failed him that afternoon by being too distracted with other things to notice his disappearance.

Why am I sharing a story about a little lost dog? Well, I realized hours later that it was connected to something important—what I'd learned while I was in the middle of my cancer treatment and learning to get in touch with the core of myself. I'd done that through guided imagery, and meditation.

Guided imagery wasn't what I thought it was when I first researched it. It's not like sports, where you envision yourself hitting a home run or crossing the finish line first. It's about allowing yourself to relax into a safe space where you can communicate with your intuition in a way that can never be done on the treadmill of life. You identify figures, people, and safe objects and communicate with them. There's a good book by Leslie Davenport on the topic called *Healing and Transformation Through Self-Guided Imagery*.

I was skeptical at first, thinking it was all a bunch of hooey. But I came to understand that, as human beings, we know a lot about ourselves. We almost always know the answer to a question, though we'll vet it over and over with others for analysis. Our intuition will tell us the answer, if we will only listen.

With practice, I learned that I could find out easily what my body needed, what my spirit needed, what I should be doing, by simply being quiet and listening to the voice within. *Don't panic*, I'd think. *Just sit. Listen. Pay attention.*

Chemo treatments were always followed by bad days. I could barely get off the couch for the first couple of days, and then I would try venturing out to the mailbox and, later, to the recycling bins. Finally, days later, I'd walk to the end of the driveway. But all the while I would consult the inner spirit I'd met through my mediations. I called her Volleyball Girl. Through guided visual imagery I learned how to get in touch with the various parts of myself that would take care of me. Volleyball Girl looked like I had at age twenty, in perfect health and physical fitness; in my meditations she was always playing beach volleyball. She represented my physical self.

While meditating, I would visit the safe haven I had created at the beach, where I would find her and others. I'd ask, "What do you need today? How are you feeling?" As crazy as it sounds, she would always tell me. If I were doing too much, she would sometimes say, "You know, I could use a little time out." I listened. I learned to listen.

I sought out that same inner voice when I was desperately seeking Zorro. I stopped and quieted myself. I grabbed the panic by the throat and hushed it, trusting that his little spirit would connect with mine. He did. We did. And the ending was a happy one.

So what's the point? Just listen. You have the answer to every question, you just need to hear it for yourself.

O Captain, My Captain

NOVEMBER 2012–JANUARY 2013

SOMETIMES, LIKE IT OR NOT, THE SUN FAILS TO SHINE. AFTER returning from my dream trip to Italy with Carole—pedaling our way from *poggio* to *poggio*, feasting on the gastronomical delights and sipping Brunello fit for royalty—I had to face reality. I sometimes compare it to a rocket returning from outer space: reentry is almost always unpleasant and uncomfortable.

After treatment ended, I had a blood test every few months to make sure my CA-125 score remained in the 0–35 normal range. At first, it hovered around 8. But that number crept slowly upward. When it was over 20, it was time for another CT scan.

Part of coping with ovarian cancer is knowing that it can come back, as the Huff had told me. I had wondered, at that time, what decisions I might have made if I had known that surgery and a full summer of chemotherapy wouldn't kill this thing. What would I have done? Faced with a very uncertain future and the real possibility that it would return, what would I do if I had to go through the whole ordeal all over again?

The news of the possibility of recurrence had been harder to bear than I let on. The Huff was such an ardent supporter and cheerleader, and I had no doubt that he and I would keep beating it back together.

I had hugged his neck and snapped a selfie of us for the blog, and then I left. I walked out of the hospital into the bright sunshine, found my way to the car some blocks away, and climbed inside. I gripped the steering wheel, working my fingers back and forth over the smooth wood. And I cried.

Having a new CT scan served as yet another reminder of the tenuous grasp I had—that we all have—on life. I understood all too well that the party could be over any minute. This was not the kind of understanding one gets through some pedestrian turn-of-phrase like, "You could die tomorrow. You could get hit by a bus." People say that all the time, but no one truly means it. People do not really believe they are going to be hit by a bus. For starters, that would require them to get out of their gas-guzzling cars and walk somewhere. But I can tell you firsthand that it is an altogether different experience to have your almost-certain death handed to you on a silver platter. That perspective adds a whole new dimension to how you spend your days.

And then, on the very day I was to have the scan he had just ordered for me, the Huff was gone.

November 7, 2012: O Captain, My Captain!

The Huff and Me in Happier Times

My doctor. My friend. My team captain. Gone is the wonderful man who not only saved my life, but who inspired me constantly with his own courage in the face of his own battle against cancer. He was diagnosed just a year before I was.

The Huff, as I came to fondly refer to him, was an expert of mine in a trial many years ago. Years had passed since then, but when I went to his office that fateful day in 2011 as a cancer patient myself, we already had a bond that made me more than just a file on his desk.

I would come to know him so much better, and I would learn that there were no "files" on his desk. His patients were immensely important to him. He returned to work sooner than most might have after his initial battle subsided, so that he could help as many people as possible. I was fortunate to have reconnected with him in this way, and I was lucky to have his guidance and amazing spirit govern my treatment.

I picked the Huff to lead my team instead of Dr. Doomsday, solely because of his positive outlook.

"We got this," he said. "Your cancer is treatable, and beatable."

I will never forget those words. And besides, what doctor will give you his personal cell phone number to text or call any time of the day or night? And his personal e-mail?

My office visits were filled with shared anecdotes and stories; we talked of travels, bicycling, and birdies on the golf course—he loved golf. He enjoyed those twilight tee times when he could stroll along hitting and chasing that little white ball. Not a visit went by where he did not tell me news of his latest birdie or par. Once, he told me he had been playing a round with his father, who was lamenting the fact that Doc was dying.

"Dying?" Doc chuckled. "I just shot a birdie! If this is dying, then it's all good."

That was his typical reaction. He was *living* with cancer, and he taught me to do the same.

He took time for special trips with his wife and young daughters to make memories that will last their lifetimes. He gave them love and attention, and gave himself the pure pleasure of a ten-foot putt.

"We all have to die at some point," he once said. "It's about enjoying your life and living until that happens." He understood, deeply, what life on this rock is all about.

The Huff exemplified everything I've ever believed about facing this awful disease. He walked the walk. He had a can-do attitude and studiously worked at being present in the moment.

Now I feel like a ship with no rudder, and the void in my life is palpable. Today I return for a CT scan, which he ordered just ten days ago when I last saw him. What will I do now, without him? What will his beautiful wife and daughters do but miss him every day? What an amazing, talented gift of a human being he was to this planet. I miss him so much already.

I'd called his office to check in on one thing or another and learned that he had been unexpectedly hospitalized due to some kind of infection. I knew he constantly had to deal with issues related to his own cancer treatment, but by and large, at least from all appearances, he had been doing just great.

Over the next several days, I called or e-mailed to see how he was doing, and each time I was disappointed and concerned to learn that he was still in the hospital. When I called late one afternoon as I left the office, one of his kind nurses broke the news to me. He was gone. I was devastated. I climbed in the car, closed the door, and wept. Without warning, that empty feeling started to envelope me. Though I had wonderful family and friends in my life, I felt alone, rudderless.

The Huff's death was a terrible loss. He had convinced me I could win, that I could beat ovarian cancer. He had inspired me, laughed with me, and taught me how to live a life beyond chronic illness. He walked the walk through his own journey and served as an example for many. He was my guide; I trusted him, and he had healed me. He was the rock against which I leaned in the face of the unknown and unknowable. The void he left behind was unmistakable and unfillable.

I shared my grief and loss with another source of strength in my life, the inimitable Raymond Himmell, my acupuncturist. He too was a long-time cancer survivor who understood all too well the physical challenges of the disease and its treatment, as well as the emotional toll it could take if allowed to run rampant. Visiting Raymond was like holding the hand of a dear friend you knew you could trust with all things. He was a treasure—a nurturer and a healer—and I was and remain grateful to him for walking me gently away from the ledge after the Huff's passing. With great kindness, he nudged me back to my own path of gratitude and healing.

And so, I kept after it— life, that is. The new year brought with it an engagement ring and the promise of excitement, love, and adventure. I vowed to begin it in the healthiest way possible, and so challenged myself to my first-ever official bicycle race as a licensed member of the USA Cycling Association.

Yes, I said *race*.

It was forty degrees the morning of January 1, 2013, when I rolled up to the start line of a three-and-a-half mile race. The San Bruno Hill

Climb is an annual event, a New Year's Day tradition for bicycle racers throughout Northern California. Though too early in the season for any great wins (or losses), it is a challenging event. It was my first real race.

Why in the world I decided at fifty-two to add racing to my favorite recreational pastime, I don't know. I must have been nuts. But chugging my way up that hill reminded me how far I'd come on my journey to recovery. Embarking on my second cancer-free year, I was grateful that I had the ability to ride my bike at all, let alone participate in an actual USA Cycling–sanctioned race. My goal for that year, and every year going forward, was to be mindfully present at whatever I was doing—whether that was pedaling up a hill, giving undivided attention to the wheel in front of me during a team time-trial event, or just enjoying the view. I was determined not to miss a single moment of what I had grown to appreciate more fully as my wonderful, gifted life.

Soon thereafter came a birthday.

Ah, birthdays. Ya love 'em or hate 'em, depending on whether cake and ice cream are involved or the candles can be blown out only with a fire extinguisher. I tolerated forty and celebrated fifty. Then I wondered whether I would actually see sixty. I still don't know. But I happily and gratefully celebrated my fifty-third trip around the sun. I saw the crisp, winter days in vivid color—the hand-knitted caps on Market Street, the seagulls soaring over the water at the Ferry Building, the man playing his trumpet while his buddy shined shoes at the end of the cable car line. People walking, rushing, getting anywhere with their cups of coffee in gloved hands. The winter days were beautiful. Each moment was beautiful. I was surrounded by friends and blessed by love and the future was bright. I was deeply grateful to be alive on this planet for each day I had left here, no matter how many that might be.

Little People Doing Little Things

OBSERVATIONS

EVER LOOK OUT THE WINDOW OF AN AIRPLANE? I DO, AND I MARVEL at the smallness of everything below. It reminds me of when I was a child playing with Matchbox cars and doll houses. Everything is so perfectly tiny.

A now-long-ago video game once beckoned me to create cities and infrastructure, building freeways, airports, and the like. The view from an airplane is similar: little people doing little things—driving fast, riding trains, walking dogs—in perfect harmony and yet autonomously. Like *The Truman Show*, it all seems so perfectly staged. The Earth churns round and round while babies cry, puppies whine, and CNN tells us more of the same bad news. Arizona glows in the desert night while a desert elsewhere is bombed for the umpteenth time.

Mini-vignettes they are—little soldiers, little houses, little everything. At home, the neighborhood lights on the hilltop beyond my window evoke a similar feeling. I love that time of night when the sun has just set and the lights flicker on one after the other. Little people in their brightly lit houses having dinner, watching television, or weeping for a loved one gone too soon. Magically attuned in harmony, yet so alone, each in his or her own way. My grasp of this smallness seems so real sometimes, as if I truly know and understand the vastness of what lies beyond. I stand in my driveway and look up. I see the world, albeit briefly, for exactly what it is. We often run like ants, don't we? How silly it all seems sometimes.

There must be more. I feel it.

Those at Steve Job's bedside when he passed reported his last words were, "Oh wow!" I ponder that, and the look on my father's face as he left this planet for his next journey: he sighed with joy, and I watched quietly as his eyes opened wide upon seeing something of great and obvious beauty. Or was it recognition? Though the room was dark, a bright light reflected from his blue-gray eyes in a moment I will never forget.

I am grateful for this seemingly spatial awareness, for it is a gift that keeps me present and alive to share and love and enjoy each minute here with the other little people, doing our little things.

On Moving On

APRIL 2013

OF ALL THE THINGS THAT HAPPENED AS I EMBARKED ON MY SECOND post-treatment year, the most painful was the loss of my dearest companion and friend—my little Zorro.

I had shared more than fifteen years of my life with him, through a divorce, the loss of both my parents, a broken leg, and, of course, my cancer diagnosis and treatment. He was there through it all—ever supportive, ever loving, ever present. He was always ecstatic to see me when I walked in the door. He slept in my bed. He dried my tears with kisses.

Those fifteen years seemed like so many more, and his passing almost broke my heart. But with it, I came to an even deeper understanding of his place—indeed my place—in the world and on the continuum of life's journey. I spent every last moment with him to the very end, giving him the unending love and gentleness that he had always given me. I rocked him in my arms and whispered words of support and encouragement, hoping to allay any misgivings he had about the path down which he would soon run. Tears streamed down my face as he drew his last breath against my chest, and I bid him adieu, kissing the top of his soft, little black and gray head.

--- ❧ ---

April 17, 2013: On Moving On

Zorro

Sometimes a spirit comes into the world that you just know from the outset is going to change things. It is a blessing and an honor to be in the presence of that kind of spirit, and it is humbling to be the one graced to share a daily life with its earthly form. My beloved Zorro is the embodiment of that kind of spirit.

Nary a passerby could look upon him without smiling, reaching down (way down) to touch his soft little head, and asking, "Is that a cat?" "How much does he weigh?" "What kind of dog is that?"

Like his size, he brought a tiny, little three-letter word with him everywhere he went. *J-O-Y.* Smiles burst around him like fireworks on the fourth of July. Being out in public with Zorro was like being with a celebrity. It was a mob scene most of the time, but without the dark glasses and paparazzi.

Zorro has had more friends over his lifetime than most
people have today on Facebook. An old timer now, he was
born before iPhones were invented. He has friends from
coast to coast and has enjoyed his last decade in what he
would describe himself if he could as the most beautiful
place in the world. California.

He stole everyone's
heart when he won the
San Francisco Halloween
costume contest in
Golden Gate Park shortly
after arriving in the
Golden State, where he
was photographed and
featured on the nightly
news sporting his little
Zorro costume, complete
with bolero and sword.

He snuck aboard Southwest Airlines before dogs were
allowed (are they now?), and still has unused Advantage
Miles on American. He has run the California beaches up
and down, scurrying away from the waves (with me chasing
behind, yelling and waving arms frantically lest he be swept
away by the tiniest of shoreline splashes), and has chased
sticks and tiny golf-ball-size tennis balls for miles and miles.
He has enjoyed many a ride in a basket on the front of my
bike, including the beautiful seventeen-mile drive in Carmel
and Monterey, and up and over the rolling hills in Woodside.
He has hiked mile after mile both on foot (ten steps to every
human one?) and in a front pack that I've worn everywhere
from Mount Tamalpais to Marin County festivals and art
fairs. He has dined in fine restaurants, enjoyed Academy

Award-winning movies at the theatre (he loves popcorn), and partied at concerts. He loves coffee and red wine. His recent years have found him just as spirited, but enjoying the finer aspects of the leisure life at Mendocino hideaways and Big Sur spas. He is a joy to hold, and behold, and has given more kisses than Hershey's will ever make.

Today he sleeps quietly, just in front of the fireplace in his snuggly soft, little bed. When he awakes, I hold him, and cry. Seems I will never be ready for the moving on of his little spirit after spending just shy of fifteen years with him. He has been my best friend and companion through some of life's greatest challenges, a constant source of unconditional love and support, and has made the world a little brighter with each smile he evoked. Coming to grips with saying good-bye to this petite package with such a big, giving soul is almost too much to bear. But I know his work here is done, as mine will be some day, and I will try to hold fast as he makes his journey to the next and grander place. I know he'll find a stick for me to throw when I get there. Life here is just too, too short, in all its forms.

April 19, 2013: Postscript

Postscript: My darling baby boy passed peacefully at home in my arms … What a love he was. Just such a sweet, sweet boy. I will miss him terribly.

> We who choose to surround ourselves with lives even
> more temporary than our own live within a fragile
> circle, easily and often breached. Unable to accept its
> awful gaps, we still would live no other way. We cherish
> memory as the only certain immortality, never fully
> understanding the necessary plan. —*Irving Townsend*

And then came the quiet. As all who have lost someone dear in their lives know too well, the place once filled is now empty of spirit, palpably silent. No more rustling and greeting when I turned the key in the lock. No more spontaneous kisses on my bare toes; no more games of fetch. Nothing but emptiness where this little but great soul once dwelled. To be faced with the very real reality of death once again was sobering. We can curse death and shake our fist at it and try desperately to wish it away, but we cannot. It is the one true thing over which none of us have any control. It will come. Our lives are made all the more bleak by the loss of those we love. It is almost an impossible task to get on with a daily existence. It seems as though the color drains from the earth, and our eyes see only gray. No sound penetrates our hearing; no thoughts or plans occupy our minds. We are filled only with the memories of death or of good times and all things past. It is impossible to contend with the notion of a future while living in the vacuum of what once was. Our lives, the survivors', feel desolate and empty. It is in this broken space that we know sorrow for what it really is. It is the unwelcome visitor that stays too long.

Zorro's passing provided yet another opportunity to find strength in myself. He had been with me through thick and thin, and now I had been left to find my way on my own. It was as though he knew it was time to go, to let me be, and that I would be okay. He had seen me through my meeting Carole, whom he adored, and he floated gently away, leaving me in her loving care for my own journey forward. As blessed as I was to have her in my life, the emptiness in my heart for that little fellow remained.

And so it was in this unhappy space that I looked up and saw the path in front of me, one that had become a path of apprehension and tentativeness and uncertainty. Another blood test followed Zorro's passing, and I feared that my CA-125 score would continue its assent beyond the normal range. The reality of that possibility set in sharp relief my movement through daily existence and the numbering of my days.

Game Changer

SPRING 2013

April 28, 2013: Game Changer

See if this sounds familiar: Stuck in a traffic jam on the way to work, only to arrive and have computer problems block your every move until lunchtime. Then, if you're lucky, you have a quick lunch with friends or a favorite colleague (or if you're not lucky, you eat at your desk). Then it's back to the grind until the whistle blows. You rush out the door, stopping at the grocery store for dinner from the deli section, then home to walk the dog, eat, feed and bathe the kids (maybe), and off to bed. You spend five minutes with the nightstand book you can never finish. Alarm reset. Sleep. Repeat. Ah, the bliss of a banal existence.

Our usual rut is such a place of comfort. It prevents us from looking up to see what is down the road. Indeed, most of us have no idea what is to come next week or even tomorrow for that matter. It is an often boring, sometimes grim way to live. Every now and then, we think about retirement or vacation, but not much else.

But game changers can strike at a moment's notice. A car accident. A divorce. A lost loved one. These tragedies usually arrive, thankfully, unannounced. How would we survive if we knew they were coming? What would we do to stop the inevitable pain? Ever wonder what it would be like to have the gift (or curse) of foresight? For cancer survivors, we frequently have both.

Today, for example, I can see a game changer just around the corner, like handwriting on the wall.

It's odd living this way, in two- to three-month increments, from blood test to blood test. With each negative test I enjoy another brief reprieve from having to deal with cancer.

"Go. Be healthy. Live!" the Huff would say.

With each passing month I get farther beyond the end of treatment, while marking time toward that enviable five-year goal of complete remission. But now, just nineteen months after my last infusion, I find myself wondering, indeed dreading, what this week's test will reveal.

I am grateful that for the last year my CA-125 tests have been in the normal range. Yet I am mindful of their slow, upward creep, which I have tried to ignore.

"Good news! Your test is still in the normal range," the nurse chirps happily when she calls. But now I sit only five points away from an abnormal result, and I wonder what that will mean.

Yes, it's possible that my body is adjusting to its new postchemo normal. It's possible that 30, my current test score, will be the upper end of the normal range at which my body naturally operates, and my score won't get any higher. I have tried to set aside the "what-ifs" that creep into my head every now and then. Ignorance is bliss. Or is it?

Cancer survivors reap many things from surviving—a different perspective on everyday life, on friends, on love, on the hereafter. It's all part of it. But one of the things we are destined to live with is the very real possibility that the life-changing event we once endured might reoccur.

I stare out yet another airplane window (I do too much of that), looking out at the smallness of it all. And I wonder what I will be thinking seven days from now. Will I be reveling in the sheer joy of a stable blood test? Or will I be facing yet another at-bat against ovarian cancer? It's hard to cope with the loss of my beloved Zorro, to focus on my professional career, or even to make wedding plans, when I know that a game changer is just around the corner.

Many, many people will have a game-changing experience next week. Those who cannot see it coming should count themselves lucky, I guess. It's better just not to know, because the anticipation of probable outcomes is a heavy burden to bear. Bless the ostrich in all of us.

It is this survivor's malady that constantly returns me to moment-by-moment living. If I spend the next hours or days worrying about the events of next week, I will miss today. Only acceptance of the fact that I am responsible for how I spend my time will get me where I need to be. My outlook is mine to choose: I can grieve, or fret, or rejoice in the warm sunshine, the fresh air, and the love that surrounds me.

For today, I will hold steady the course. And breathe.

The second year after treatment I found myself once again facing the possibility of another battle with my internal intruder. In many ways, I had anticipated this moment. The Huff's earlier confession about the possibility of recurrence was ever-present in my mind. And now the periodic blood test would reveal any returning proliferation of the cancerous cells. What would happen next was anyone's guess, but it seemed only a matter of time before something would have to be done before the battle turned into a war, and the war would be lost.

And then it was confirmed. It was back.

Hope

MAY 2013

A DEAR FRIEND SHARED WITH ME A FEW WORDS WRITTEN BY PEMA Chodron, a Tibetan Buddhist nun:

> We think that the point is to pass the test or to overcome the problem, but the truth is that things don't really get solved. They come together and they fall apart. Only to the extent that we expose ourselves over and over to annihilation can that which is indestructible in us be found.

And so I marched ahead, with hope, despite the disappointing news.

There's always hope, isn't there? It's part of our nature to be hopeful human beings, no matter how dire the circumstances. There are people who live in war-torn and ravaged countries who manage to survive each day with the hope that somehow tomorrow things will take a turn for the better. Their glimmer of hope is so slight, and yet it persists. That glimmer exists in all of us. Somewhere.

In medicine, and with cancer in particular, those glimmers come frequently, and shine brightly. There are so many new clinical trials underway. Carole works in the medical field and is continually scouring journals and the Internet for new targeted therapies for ovarian cancer. One day, one of these therapies will end this disease forever. It's only a matter of time. And time is what survival is all about. My end game was no different from that of others who had gone before me: survive until there is a cure.

I read an article in a magazine recently about actress Valerie Harper (a.k.a. Rhoda), who has been diagnosed with incurable brain cancer. Of the many things she said, I found one particular observation especially true: "Cancer makes real what we try to obscure from ourselves." She is so right. The face-slapping reality of one's own mortality has an uncanny way of refocusing you on the task at hand: living. The past is past, and the future may never come. There is only the here and now, this moment.

Following a week of deeply contemplating what this new reality meant, I chose once again to pursue joy, not gloom. That is probably the single most important thing I would share with a cancer patient, with anyone, really. Pursue joy. You have a life to be lived and shared; you must grow and learn. You must participate. Do not give up until your body forces you to do so. Take care of your body, help it with its battle. Be conscientious. Be aware. And be joyful.

May 14, 2013: The Right to Be Joyful

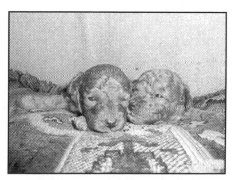

Madeleine and Madison

Poodles. Ridiculously cute, adorable, darling little bundles of warmth and goodness and life. It's difficult to explain how I ended up with them, but I will try.

After fifteen years together, not a day passes that I do not think of, and miss, my little Zorro. If I ponder too long, tears fill my eyes, and that empty space in my heart opens a bit wider. I want him back so much! The first days without him were without relief, as anyone who has ever loved a companion animal knows. All the wishing and wanting and bargaining just won't bring them back. Our time with them on this planet has passed, never to be forgotten, but sealed beautifully as if under a glass dome, never to be changed. Memories—that is all we have left.

But I don't think we are meant to be alone. People yearn for community, for friendships, for connection with others. It's in our nature to seek out those with whom we can share a laugh or a tear or a cup of coffee. We suffer through the loss of loved ones in our lives, and we go on. We are not meant to be alone, but rather, to move forward.

One night recently I read a Buddhist passage reminding us that we have the right to be joyful. We, the living. We, the human beings walking this planet. We, the caregivers and lovers and friends and flesh-and-blood bodies that awake with each new day. We, with the still-beating hearts. I fell asleep pondering this truth, and awoke thinking again about my baby Zorro, and missing him so deeply.

I wondered aloud what would have happened had I died first? What would I have wanted for him? The answer was clear: I would want for him to be loved and well cared for. Happy with his new companion, perhaps missing me even. But with great certainty I knew, even if it meant forgetting me altogether as time passed, I would want him to be happy. Deeply happy and content and safe and filled with joy each day of his little, tiny life. I would want him to move forward.

As much as I longed to snuggle the little face in the photograph on my bedside table, I knew then and there that he wanted the same for me. I felt. I understood.

Oh, the times he ran to my side when I was sad, demanding that I pick him up so he could lick the tears from my face. He would find me anywhere in the house if he heard me crying. His beautiful little wiggle greeted me at the front door each day. He always seemed to be smiling. He brought me such joy. And now I understood that he would want me to be joyful, not to wallow and wade in the darkest of places, wanting only his return and nothing more. Wanting what could never be. Our time together was done, and I will cherish it always. But only I could stop the pain, and only by moving on. I understood it was no dishonor to my darling boy to relish the life we had together but to release the grief of his passing so that I could see a new day on the horizon. I must go on without him. He would want that, even as he continued to live in my heart.

And so that morning as I lay in bed, contemplating a new beginning, I began a search for a different little friend to bring into my life. Someone with whom I could write a different chapter. A precious little light, pure and gentle, to soften my numbered days. Someone to care for. Someone to bring the joy back to my quiet homecomings.

Enter Madeleine and her brother, Madison, two darling, weeks-old teacup poodles. They are plenty ridiculous. Teacup poodles, truly red ones, aren't easy to find. But they represent another new beginning, the sharing of new experiences, the making of new memories.

Forward. It is the only direction I can go.

And so, with my blood-test score squarely rooted in the abnormal range, I made my way to the hospital with great trepidation for a visit with my new doctor. They summon you for these things, of course. They want to catch it early, just as the Huff had said. We were catching it. I should have been glad, though I wasn't. Not really.

I sat waiting, not in a paper gown but in a white hospital robe with a red, embroidered logo. The room seemed smaller than last time; the walls a bit colder; the fancy computer monitors and machines a bit more ominous. I would soon know the details of a most recent CT scan, which would reveal the location of the growing tumor that was causing the increase in cancer antigens in my blood. I took deep breaths, and stared at my fingernails.

Although Carole was seated in a chair right beside me, I avoided her eyes. She too was concerned. But I had seen that helpless look before in the eyes of others, and I did not want to see it in hers. We waited together in silence.

Then the door cracked open and in he walked.

"Good morning!" Dr. Jonathan Berek welcomed me with outstretched arms. "You look terrific," he said with a ready hug.

I liked this guy.

When battling cancer, you had better be smarter than the cancer. And that meant getting the smart people on your side. Carole found Dr. Berek for me. He was the chair of Stanford's Department of Obstetrics and Gynecology and the director of the Women's Cancer Center there. He was my new team captain, but we were just getting to know each other. This was only the second time we had met.

In addition to being on top of all the new developments in cancer treatments and generally the go-to guy on gynecological cancers, he was also super nice, sincerely and authentically nice. His affable personality reminded me a lot of the Huff, but he was older and had less hair. Not that hair matters, but what was left of his was kind of charming in that academic sort of way. He exuded warmth and confidence, and I had trusted him upon our first meeting.

Kind though he was, I sat there dreading the news and steeling myself for the worst. Then, as matter-of-fact as possible, he explained my current predicament.

"Your CT scan from last week revealed small evidence of returning disease in one of your lymph nodes."

Returning disease, I repeated silently. He had said the dreaded words out loud.

My lymph nodes were the genesis of my original metastases, somewhere in my abdomen, before the cancer had spread so far that I finally noticed the swollen node in my neck. Here again, he explained, the swollen lymph node was deep within my abdomen, externally undetectable.

"Node growth, plus a nominally abnormal CA-125 test means the cancer cells are likely starting to grow again and it's time for more cancer treatment," he explained.

I looked at Carole then as my eyes grew wet. Our wedding was four months away, and I just couldn't stomach the notion of a bride on chemo. Argh.

There was no known cure for ovarian cancer. It was all about trying to keep the cells under control and stabilized. Carole knew this as well as I did, and she had already begun her lobbying effort for a second round of chemotherapy to destroy the cells before their growth became uncontrollable.

I waited a moment or two before asking, "What are my choices?" pretending to be as matter-of-fact as everyone else in the room, and also pretending like I *had* a choice.

What I didn't know was that I *did* have a choice.

We discussed, negotiated actually, further chemo treatment,

alternatives, and timing. Carole was practically adamant about the chemo, but Dr. B was steadfastly on my side and more than willing to talk her down from the ledge. He had an idea.

"How about we try Letrozole?" he offered.

"What's that?" I asked.

"A pill," he replied., "We sometimes use it with patients who have had breast cancer as a preventative from reoccurrence."

Just a pill? I was shocked, but elated.

Letrozole was an estrogen inhibitor, and ovarian cancer cells apparently love estrogen. Thrive on it, in fact. Dr. B was willing to try the pill on me, and I was willing to take it. It took some doing to convince Carole that I shouldn't submit to chemo right away, but with the game set as two against one, she finally relented.

I would take the little yellow pill over the following months until after the wedding; then I'd have another CT scan and blood test to see if it was keeping the cancer cells at bay.

Practically giddy, I gladly took the prescription and skipped out of the hospital.

Yep, I liked this guy.

Short-Term Living

JULY–SEPTEMBER 2013

I CAME TO BETTER UNDERSTAND MY LONG-TERM PROGNOSIS, WHICH was that I would spend the rest of my life managing my cancer until a cure was found. Fortunately, the research into ovarian cancer treatment had exploded in recent years, and the possibilities on the horizon were amazing. Until then, I had decided, my cancer and I would just continue to live a happy and healthy life together. I promised to play nice and not nuke the shit out of it so long as it promised not to try and kill me. In legal speak, it seemed that we had reached an accord, for the time being, anyway.

The months passed as my acceptance of living in multi-month segments began to grow. Any minute, it seemed, the other shoe would drop, and my score would be off the charts, warranting another round of treatment. But oddly, I had grown comfortable with this segmented living. It served an important purpose, which was to keep me grounded in the present and serve as a reminder that my days here are numbered. They are with us all, I suppose, though most of us don't spend our days thinking about the limit. This segmented living continually prompted me to take stock of my life and what I was doing with it. It also piqued my curiosity about the why and how of our existence and what might come after.

A dear friend of mine from New York visited and left with me a book he had been reading. *Proof of Heaven* was a remarkable account of the self-described "near-death experience" of Eben Alexander, a neurosurgeon. Alexander tells the story of mysteriously contracting a deadly bacterial meningitis that placed him in a seven-day coma, during which his soul transcended his body to experience the afterlife and commune with the universe. It was a dazzling and detailed confirmation of what I have pondered for some time, but never heard told in such a compelling way. I had briefly read about similar things before in Dr. Brian Weiss's book, *Many Lives, Many Masters*. Weiss describes learning of his patients' near-death experiences (or past-life experiences) through a series of regression therapy sessions.

In any event, finishing Alexander's book caused me to contemplate, yet again, what my higher self is supposed to be doing on this planet during the fifteen minutes we've each been given here. It's an age-old question, for certain, but I couldn't stop asking it. *What is my purpose here? Am I being all I can be? What am I to learn on this journey? How much longer do I have? Will I get it done before I'm gone, whatever "it" is?* In my humble view, these questions warrant more than the five to ten minutes or so we give them every few weeks while driving to work and between our mental list making.

I reconsidered attending a weekend meditation retreat in the hills of Northern California. Perhaps some designated time to think deep thoughts and contemplate my connection with the universe would help me to better understand the mystery of my being here.

I know with a certainty there is much more to our existence than the workaday world. But our societal structure isn't necessarily conducive to existing comfortably while also realizing our deepest and truest potential. Would that we could all shed the heavy yoke of responsibility and just be. Sometimes just being is exactly what we need to know our truth and more fully realize our life's journey.

Magic

SEPTEMBER 2013

AFTER BLITHELY SKIPPING AWAY FROM MY CANCER PROBLEMS FOR awhile, the magical month finally came: Carole and I would marry.

September 9, 2013: Looking Back, Looking Forward

Photo courtesy of Christopher Gage.

Two years ago today I spent nine hours with a frozen turban on my head trying to survive the last, and worst, day of chemo. The relief as that day drew to a close was almost overwhelming, and it brings tears to my eyes to think back on that time, and I wonder how I ever got through it. But we do, don't we? We just buckle down, eyes forward, and plunge straight ahead in times like those—focused on the end of the tunnel.

Ah, the end of the tunnel. It propels us forward when at times it seems that all is lost. It is the hope that sustains us. Hope that things will be better; it often feels like hope against hope during our darkest hours. Hope that we will, once again, have our lives back as we knew them. But we don't understand, during the dismal times, that our lives before are gone. It is then almost impossible to appreciate the changes that are taking place inside, in your heart and deepest soul, until you finally do emerge into the sunlight—polished and shiny and with more wisdom than before, somehow.

The end of my tunnel brought me the bonus round of my life, and with it a wonderful and beautiful soul with whom I am about to embark on a journey to the end of my days. Though she claims not to have noticed my lack of eyebrows when we first met, I remain skeptical. But along with my skepticism is my gratefulness that the universe allowed our paths to cross, and that my bout with cancer did not scare her away. Couples rarely know what lies in store as they embark on life's journey together, and it is the unknown surprises that frequently rend relationships. I have never known someone so brave as to walk directly into the fire as this woman has, and I love her for that, and for so very much more.

Today I look forward to sharing the rest of my life with a love so rare, and so true, that it takes my breath away. I cannot believe my good fortune. And I know that when the tunnel comes again—and it will, because life is like that—I will walk through it hand in hand with her.

⚜

That amazing woman with nerves of steel and a heart of gold, who paraded fearlessly and straight into my anemic, lashless life, graced me with "I do." Of all the things she said to me during our wedding, the thing I will never forget is this: "My love is not fragile. It will not leave you."

I'm counting on that.

Sharks

OCTOBER 2013

I HAD CAREFULLY SCHEDULED MY NEXT BLOOD TEST TO TAKE PLACE after the wedding. There were so many other things to do running up to that special day that I had no time to contemplate the possible results or outcomes. Indeed, I always tried very hard not to spend time doing that, because fretting or worrying or contemplating or anticipating is a useless waste of time. The results would be either good or bad, or somewhere in-between, but either way, my angst about the outcome of a blood test would serve no useful purpose.

Nonetheless, I am human. And there are times when my predicament awareness floats too close to the surface. Sometimes it's just impossible to ignore, and it's the awareness itself that brings me back to the moment.

And then there's denial, that sweet, sweet respite from the not-so-good news in life. A place of comfort and solitude. Peaceful. Serene. Like floating on a raft in the sun-drenched, salty ocean while the surf pounds the shore twenty yards away. You bob up and down, back and forth—utterly content. Sharks? What sharks? Just another beautiful day, isn't it?

Life is good when the biggest decision of the day is, what's for lunch? Or when your only problem is finding a flat tire while rushing to the office, or locking your keys in the car in the middle of running errands in your oh-so-organized world.

But the sharks ... they circle, don't they?

Cancer is like that for me: a circling shark. It is an ever-present threat lingering just below the glittery surface of life. A big, fat dose of mortality that won't go away, but which is utterly ignored most days while wedding celebrations and vacations are planned. I can live with it, treat it, or just deny it. To be sure, the danger of the latter is my own untimely end. Ultimately, I must face it, and do something about it. Or not.

There are many things in life like this. Certainly health issues; if you deny they exist, they will only get yuckier. What about relationship issues? Denying and sweeping things under the rug will only result in festering resentment that will fly out in a rage months from now.

This is the part of life that, to twist a Facebook phrase, I "unlike" very much, as do we all, I suppose. It's the dealing with the unpleasantness of important things that demand our attention; the unwanted or unpleasantly unexpected. It's the un-fun part of living, without which the fun parts would surely seem bland.

And so it was that the danger continued circling just below the surface of everyday life as my blood test score continued rising, now eleven points higher than the time before and hanging like a lantern high above the normal range. But like a shark bumping my raft then swimming away, I was again spared the fate of dropping into the abyss of cancer treatment.

Hallelujah!

My follow-up visit to see the good Dr. Berek brought the great news that my CT scan had not changed since June. There was no change at all. Despite my rising test score, things remained at status quo, leaving just me and my little pill heading into the holidays. Living life in multi-month increments provided a level of intensity that I have not yet fully mastered. I hoped to settle into the rhythm one day. Meanwhile, it did keep life fresh and very focused.

Another Trip Around the Sun

JANUARY 2014

WELCOME, BIRTHDAY. GLAD TO SEE YOU AGAIN.

As we completed another trip around the sun, I gratefully settled into the beginning of yet another post-treatment year and celebrated my third bonus birthday. They would all be bonuses, as far as I was concerned, since I wouldn't be having them but for the advent of modern medicine.

On my fifty-third birthday, I found myself working a twelve-hour day—not quite what I had hoped or planned to do. Yet, as with every other day, I was torn between the desire to keep a roof over my head, or jettison it all and live off my savings until it ran out. The gamble, of course, was whether I would outlive my savings. Modern medicine, with all its benefits, could just make that happen. Who knew? But if not, I would be awfully upset if I had spent the last years of my life toiling away.

When I started complaining about work, I would recall those chemo days where I longed for the mundanity of a regular workday. That said, an early retirement would have been most welcome.

For those of us in the American workforce, the rat race is just a few steps out the front door. The time clock, the traffic, the crowded train, the long lines at the airport (unless you get the free pass from the TSA). The clients, the demands, the endless string of things to do. Overworked and overwhelmed at times with the never-ending obligations, I would realize I had not really sat and meditated for months. Could that be right? There are countless articles on the need to relax and make free time. Everyone knows stress will kill you. If you don't believe me, just stop right now and take a breath and feel what stress does to your body. Not good; certainly not good for me.

A few days after my birthday had come and gone, I played hooky. I stopped, slept in, got up late, lingered over a homemade latté, and thought about my life, what it meant to be me, and how I was living my journey on Earth.

Existence is a long continuum. Life is so brief. Each year is a gift, and I was determined not to waste it. I would love, I would laugh, and I would live each new day with gratefulness.

And yes, I would still go to work.

Urgent Living

FEBRUARY 2014

Still suffering from professional lethargy and not wanting to spend most of my waking hours watching my life ebb away in six-minute billing increments, I languished in no-man's-land before shifting my focus to new challenges, new adventures, new learning.

That's when the inspiration to write this book, to share my experiences with others, began to grow and take shape. Although it had been in the back of my mind since the plane ride home from Italy, my thoughts now went to it more often than not. It was something I should do, needed to do, had to do. Despite my own reluctance to join support groups, the urge to share even a smidgeon of hope with someone who might need it overcame my desire to keep close to the vest my very personal experience of survival.

I felt a sense of urgency, likely propelled by an ever-increasing blood test score, which now fell just shy of 100. I wanted to retire, not because I was lazy, but because I was anxious to spend my days doing something other than reading briefs and arguing with lawyers. People sue each other over the most ridiculous things, and unfortunately, I was exposed to their frivolity almost daily. It often seemed like such a waste of time and energy. I thought my time would be better spent with my beautiful wife and friends and doing the things that fed my soul. There seemed to be so little time.

One random day I was up before five in the morning and on my way to work. Eureka! There could be more hours in the day! Of course, that would require less sleep. But you just can't have it both ways, although heaven knows I tried. There was so much living to be done and such a short time remaining; at least it felt that way.

Then came more not-as-good-as-it-could-have-been news. I managed to get myself to the Stanford Cancer Center for a BRCA1 test. Almost everyone likely has heard about this test by now since Angelina Julie made public her decision to have a double mastectomy.

BRCA1 is the genetic test that uncovers the gene change in a person's DNA string that predicts breast or ovarian cancer. I use the word "change" rather than "defect" since that is apparently the cool, politically correct, medical lingo these days.

Turns out that, I have a 60 percent chance of developing breast cancer, since I've already had ovarian cancer. It was that gene change that was responsible for my ovarian cancer. My mother was a carrier, as am I. Had I known this fifteen years ago I could have had a prophylactic hysterectomy and avoided cancer altogether. Hindsight—not so helpful.

Because of a long history of cancer on my mother's side, the nice geneticist made sure to tell me it "wasn't my fault" that I had ovarian cancer. Present since birth, it takes time to develop, which is why most ovarian cancers don't show up until women are in their forties or fifties.

Interesting, I thought, that she was compelled to assuage any fear I had about causing my cancer. That had never occurred to me. It didn't seem to be something I might blame myself for, like a hangover, for example. Apparently I didn't have the typical reaction to the news that most women have, which can range from mild hysteria to a complete meltdown. It just seemed like another data point in my medical file and nothing more. My meltdown had long since come and gone. Nonetheless, it was a relief to know that I did, in fact, actually have *something* in common with Angelina.

It seems that Angie and I are in a very select group because only a tiny percentage of the world population is BRCA1 positive. My group is even smaller because only about 15 percent of all women diagnosed with ovarian cancer are BRCA1 positive. This latter point really is a lucky break because BRCA1 carriers generally have a longer and better response to chemotherapy than non-BRCA1 carriers. In addition, there are many clinical trials developing and testing targeted therapies (read: cure?) for women exactly like me: BRCA1 positive, in their fifties, and with a high fitness profile.

"This is probably the reason your blood-test numbers are just now beginning to creep up three years after your diagnosis, compared to six months afterward," the good Dr. Berek said when I checked in with him after the test. "BRCA1 carriers also respond well to subsequent treatment," he added.

I feared that treatment might soon be coming to a theater near me if the little pill stopped working. I wasn't looking forward to a Penguin Cap sequel, though I hoped maybe round two would be different somehow. Doctor B said maybe only the Carboplatin next time.

Only?

Whatever.

Meanwhile, I turned my attention back to living and decided to get serious about my crazy idea to be a bicycle racer.

After my first stutter start at racing on my own, I was fortunate enough to meet a terrific group of women on a Northern California bike-racing team who invited me to join them. Mostly, they wanted Carole, who had raced with them for many years already (though on competing teams) and whom they had been courting for some time. I was the tagalong. But once invited, I committed to giving my very best in the sport I loved, and to performing at a much higher level than ever before. After a quarter century of recreational group rides, fundraising events, and multi-day marathons, I hired a cycling coach to teach me to race. Did I mention I was fifty-four? It was lunacy, sheer lunacy.

News flash: racing is really, really hard. The only thing harder than the racing itself is the training. It requires discipline day in and day out, stick-to-itiveness, and sheer will power. It's harder than dating, dieting, going to work, or most of the other things I'd tried. It was tough training while also holding down a full-time job and having a family; okay, it does help if your spouse also races. Some dark mornings along the foggy banks of San Francisco Bay, as I ramped up my heart rate just shy of the puke zone, I'd ask myself, *What was I thinking?*

My utter empathy with Olympic athletes grew; not that I was ever one, but I could only imagine the level of dedication it takes to become the best in the world. Me? I was just trying to avoid embarrassing my teammates at the start/finish line.

Yes, training was hard. But funnily enough, once you beat back cancer almost everything else pales by comparison. When I was exhausted, it only took a nanosecond to remember my inability to get up off the couch after chemo. The word *can't* quickly disappears from your vocabulary, because you *can*. There are few things that provide the same level of self-confidence one gets from donning a flak jacket and marching directly to the front lines of cancer treatment, guns a-blazin'. You can tick that notch on the benefits totem.

Even as I trudged along day by day, workout after workout, I stayed focused on killing those cancer cells. The geneticist had told me exercise prevented cancer recurrence, and I'd also read somewhere that cancer cells cannot survive in an oxygenated environment. Though I wasn't clear on the medical ins and outs of such a theory, in my mind's eye cancer cells were perishing with each elevated heart rate and gasping breath. I was killing those pesky little bastards one at a time. The longer I stayed in the "pain cave," as they call it in racing, the more cancer cells were dying. Although that was my vision, I had no empirical evidence to prove its truth. I entertained only wishful thinking that my next blood test would reveal anything other than the continued, incremental climb higher and higher.

Soon I would be shocked.

In April 2014, just two months after beginning my training program, I received some amazing news. Though still in the abnormal range, my CA-125 score had dropped eighteen points. Now, I had no idea if that was medically significant, but I did know this number had crept only upward for the last two-and-a-half years. Only twice, and then only in small increments, had the number ever decreased. The tests were performed by the same lab every time, so there was no variance based on lab-testing protocols.

The only thing I did differently between February and April was hire a cycling coach who put me to work almost every day. Recalling my earlier meeting with the geneticist, I became convinced that exercise really did have an impact on cancer-cell growth. Either that, or I was engaged in fantasy thinking once again. In addition, the "kitten scan" (my more palatable term for the CT scan) showed only an infinitesimal increase in size of that naughty lymph node somewhere in my abdomen.

I e-mailed the test results to Dr. Berek. "What do you think, Doc? Steady as she goes?"

"Absolutely," he replied. "Steady as she goes."

I was both surprised and deliriously happy to get yet another reprieve from being a cancer patient. I never liked that label anyway.

Upon Leaving

SUMMER 2014

LIKE IT OR NOT, I THINK ABOUT DEATH THESE DAYS. A LOT. NOT IN A bad way, as that statement surely implies, but rather in a matter of fact way. Death is more real than concept now. Though I am not preoccupied with it, having faced it as an absolute— that is, if you don't do something about your cancer, it *will* kill you—thinking about death reminds me that my days here are limited. It is probably the reason that I also constantly think about retirement. My wife likely is quite tired of hearing me say, "I don't want to work until I die." It's a sentiment that most people can relate to, no doubt. We're all just sick to death of working day in and day out with little more relief than a two-week vacation now and then, if we're lucky. Some have managed to steer their lives away from the drudgery into the arts or other, more sustaining occupations, but the rest of us are filing briefs, washing cars, and cleaning toilet bowls. Some days it feels like we are doing all three things at once.

But now and then come thoughts of death that simmer somewhere between the esoteric what's-life-all-about and retirement planning. What will the actual moment of death be like? Where will I be? Who will be there with me? Anyone? Dying can be so different; sometimes it comes as a surprise, sometimes it lingers on and on. What if you could choose your exit point? I don't mean that in a suicidal way, the often tragic end to deep depression; I mean, when you're just done with it all, whether it be a lingering illness or simply old age. What if?

An acquaintance of mine made this choice, and her decision stayed with me for days and weeks. She had been ill, with cancer, for a long period of time. I swear it's going to kill us all. But near the end, told she had three or so months to live, she decided it was time to go. Blessedly, she lived in a state with a Death with Dignity law. She made an appointment, and then at a certain day and time, she was gone.

Knowing about her decision weighed on me. The day before, I thought about her constantly—imagining her enjoying her last sunset, watching a hummingbird at the window for the final time, smelling her last rose. I wondered how she could move through the day knowing she would be dead by noon of the next. And I cried for her husband, who loved her so, distraught at the tortured motions of waking the following morning and counting the minutes until she passed.

To make a statement not too profound, death is so, well, final. And the great weight of moving on is left to the shoulders of those who remain. Perhaps the only good that comes from a scheduled good-bye is that those you hold dear have an opportunity to make things right, to say what's in their hearts, and to bid you farewell. They have a chance to come to their own terms of life without you. I struggled with understanding her choice, and yet I understood it completely. Sometimes it's just time. And when it is, bravery comes naturally to the departing and less so to those left behind.

July 7, 2014: Upon Leaving

And then there are those times when the march through
the day comes to a screeching halt. When the planet
stops turning, if only for a moment, or a day, or a week. It
happens when you lose someone you love.

A dear friend has lost a loved one to cancer, and I was deeply saddened by the news. I hate that cancer has once

again wrapped itself around someone's life and taken her away.

Death. It's a part of life we all avoid discussing, but which is utterly essential to our very existence. Surrounded with so many unknowns, it remains clouded in mystery, dread, and fear. And yet it is inevitably a returning to our truer selves.

There is a song to which I am drawn each time I hear it, particularly when sung by k.d. lang and Jane Siberry. Upon the occasion of my own passing, I have asked that it be played at whatever life celebration may follow. When I think about my own battle with cancer, and when (or if) it will escalate once again, I contemplate the end of my days with some sense of relief knowing that the finish line of this great rat race will finally be crossed. No more toiling day after day for money. No more taxes. No more debt, or illness, or loss. No more hatred and crime and killing sprees recounted on the daily news. No more war in Syria, or Iraq, or beyond. No more political strife and bickering and ridiculousness. No more Facebook (hallelujah!). But what will that moment be like? How much time do you spend thinking about it? Not much, I'd wager. Yet it is one of, if not the, most important moments in your life.

Ms. Siberry's words ring especially true to me; perhaps you'll agree:

Oh, and every day you gaze upon the sunset
With such love and intensity
Why, it's almost as if you could only crack the code
You'd finally understand what this all means
Oh, but if you could, do you think you would
Trade it all, all the pain and suffering?
Oh, but then you would've missed the beauty of
The light upon this earth and the sweetness of leaving

Ah, the sweetness of leaving … Every time I hear these words I think about the last good-bye. The last seeing and knowing of the familiar—of this place, of the love I have known, of the things I have seen. Of all that is earthly. I remember all too well the look in my own father's eyes as he left this world and transcended most serenely into the light. I saw it. I watched him go there, and I know what I saw. He returned to the utmost center of himself and his core being, and I thank him for giving me that precious moment of understanding. That experience has comforted me during these last years without him.

Ah, the sweetness of leaving. Perhaps sweet for the departing, but all too difficult for those left behind.

Musings

SUMMER 2014

---— ⚜ —---

June 3, 2014: Jack and I

He sits at the water's edge waiting for his ride to work. He writes something, I cannot tell what. He glances up and nods hello as I pass. He's an acquaintance and fellow commuter who still makes the daily trek to his office and back again. His name is Jack.

He's ninety-three.

I've learned a lot from Jack over the years that we've been commuting to work together, though I've never told him so directly. I should. We talk and laugh and banter back and forth about the day's events or, more often, bicycling. He was an avid bicyclist in his day, one of the better bicycle-polo players. In fact, when I first met him about fifteen years ago he was still riding his bicycle to work, pant leg rolled up on one side. He would stop for coffee at the café next door to my office, and I would watch him out the window as he enjoyed his morning repast and the newspaper. Then off he would go to his secret hideout of books and prints and all things artistic that he so loves. He's traveled, made books, taken photographs, had gallery shows featuring his work, and married the love of his life. A perfect life? Doubtful. But a full one.

Nowadays he pretends to be "the grumpy old man" on the boat, but an actor he's not. The daily flower in his lapel gives him away. I get him. He understands life. The real meaning of true enjoyment, gratefulness, and being present to experience the wonders all around us. Once a few years ago he spent days if not weeks preparing me for my bicycle tour through Tuscany. "Ride gently; take wine and bread and cheese. Stop in a meadow in the midst of your journey and enjoy," he would say. And when I returned he poured over my pictures from Italy, reliving much of his own experience from his younger years.

I race my bicycle these days, for which he frequently chastises me. "Oh ..." he'll say, "you are just so competitive. You should stop and smell the roses."

He is right, of course, and I let him go on because he is sharing a philosophy with which I deeply agree. In his own way, with his own experience, I know he understands that the roses sometimes come in the form of achieving goals once thought impossible. Experiencing the gratitude for the sheer ability to see the roses in the first place is also a way of smelling them. He understands. We agree, Jack and I.

———————————— ⚜ ————————————

Staying true to the wisdom gained from having cancer is an ongoing process. It's easy to get swept away by the tide of to-dos. Constantly cultivating an awareness of the present is key to making the most of each day left on this planet. But I've found that just being here is key: experiencing whatever is happening around me at the moment; keeping a perspective. These are the things that nurture the soul.

Out on a bike ride one morning I reveled in the sunshine on the east side of the peninsula, while it remained dismally foggy on the west side. I wondered what it must be like to live in one of the luxury homes atop the hill, with a view of all compass points at once. I imagined myself sitting in a sunny kitchen enjoying a cup of coffee, then later, on the deck, toasting the setting sun with a glass of wine. For a moment, I was envious of those who slept under that roof.

Then I thought about a blog post a friend had shared a few days earlier about her second visit to the doctor's office for a biopsy following a sketchy mammogram. She wrote about her anxiety, her fear, and her relief that she was not diagnosed with cancer. She wrote about her new understanding and empathy for other friends who had not been so lucky and that she was so very grateful for her health.

I posted a comment: "Stay grateful. Each day is a gift." I meant it, every word.

And so that day, on that morning ride, I was reminded once again that I don't need anything. I have my health, I have the love of a wonderful spouse and a terrific family (of choice and of origin), I have a great career, and I live in the most beautiful place in the world. It matters not that it isn't a four-thousand-square-foot home furnished to the hilt with beautiful objects. Those things don't matter. All that matters is that I am alive and well and able to enjoy my day and share laughter and love with those I hold dear. I am blessed to have a roof over my head and food in the fridge. Many people have neither of those things, and they have nary a thought about what they might be missing by not living in a luxury home with a view. Indeed, my own tiny condo perched on the hillside would be luxurious enough, they'd say. Perspective; that's all it takes.

As I've come full circle, or at least a good way around the darn thing, I have realized the urging of my friends meant this book should become a reality. Tentative at first, I ultimately embraced the notion of sharing my story with the hope that just one person will read it and take away something useful. I hope you are that person.

September 17, 2014: 48,809 Words

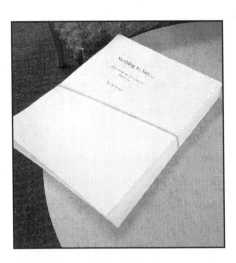

There's a reason I haven't posted very much to my blog lately. Here it is: 250 pages and 48,809 words of the initial draft of a manuscript for my first-ever book (gulp), currently titled *Nothing to Say: Observations of a Cancer Survivor.*

Because of your encouragement and responses to my blog posts, I have taken the giant leap of putting pen to paper to share my journey from diagnosis to recovery. What started on a plane ride in 2012 has finally mutated into something of substance. I hope that my story will help and inspire others who are battling this ever-increasing plague on humankind. As my mother used to say, "Lord willin' and the creek don't rise," it will be released in 2015.

My endeavor has been a well-kept secret until now for fear of not finishing it, fear of failure, fear of exposing my life and feelings to strangers, and fear of ... who knows what.

But you know what? It's just fear and nothing more. And nothing stands in the way of things the way fear does. I obviously needed to be reminded about my October 2012 post: "Don't fear the fear. It's part of what makes us human."

Here's a tidbit you may not know. This blog is not searchable on the Internet. Practically speaking, only those with a link to it or who search for it by its exact name can find it. Despite that, and the fact that I have only a handful of followers and about forty e-mail subscribers, this blog has received over 7,475 hits from Canada to Malaysia, Germany, United Kingdom, Italy, Poland, China, Columbia, and France, in addition to the United States. This tells me that there are people out there searching for information about cancer and for ways to learn from our shared experience. Because of this, I am hopeful that *Nothing to Say* will bring an element of courage in place of fear to those who are engaged in battle. I am hopeful that it will bring laughs instead of tears. I am hopeful that it will bring what it is designed to bring—a positive view on living with cancer—to those who face a life with an uncertain future ...

Trying to make sense of a cancer diagnosis is impossible. But ironically, cancer has brought many good things to my life that I would not otherwise have experienced, things that I have on occasion shared with all of you. I am willing to "go vulnerable" to others with the hope that they can derive something useful from my experience as they deal with their own struggles.

I know I can count on you, because I already have. Thank you for your ongoing support of me and of this project. Together, we can open up and do something to make a difference in people's lives.

Stay tuned.

Love,
Mockster

———————————— ⚜ ————————————

The Takeaway

TODAY

People often ask how I was able to cope with my diagnosis and treatment. The answer is as simple as it is complicated. For the most part, I ignored it. What does that mean? It means that I took steps to treat it, and then I basically ignored it and went on living my life. I didn't spend each day fretting and worrying about having cancer. Now, don't get me wrong—of course I thought about it. It just wasn't part of my every waking moment. There comes a point when you can only do so much. The treatment will either work, or it won't. But fretting and worrying and stressing yourself out won't help you; in fact, it can only do harm. Enjoying your life is the key to fighting cancer.

What has changed? Well, for starters, I don't save things the way I once did. You know that wonderful bottle of wine you've been saving for a special occasion? Drink it. Don't wait. You want to go to Italy? Go. Don't take for granted that you have another day or another year or another ten years to enjoy the bounty of planet Earth. See things and people; really look at them. Spend time doing what you love, with those you love. Feed your soul. Even if, like me, you have to continue working, try to do what you enjoy. Or if you can't do that, try to find some measure of pleasure in doing what you must. We all want to quit our jobs and become travel writers, run that bed-and-breakfast, make an independent film, or just relax. We all have that dream of escaping the monotony that is the workaday world, at least those of us who are not in the now-famous 1 percent. But most of us can't just quit, at least not unless we are holding a winning lottery ticket. We must go on. Each new day brings new encounters, new experiences, and new enlightenment about the ridiculousness of it all.

Life is ridiculous. And it's so short. Don't waste it on things that don't matter. That's what I'd tell people. Don't fret over your spouse's socks on the floor or the dishes left in the kitchen sink. That just doesn't matter. What matters is that they love you with all their heart and you them. There's a refrigerator magnet slogan that says "Don't sweat the small stuff." Those are words to live by.

If you see me out and about one of these days, please stop me. Say hello. Tell me if you loved this diatribe or hated it. Tell me what mattered and what didn't. Tell me who you are. Engage me. Engage others. Learn. Express. Believe—in yourself, in love, and in life. *Live.*

Epilogue

So, you may be wondering why I changed the title of the book. It happened—literally—at the very last minute. I had long since decided that *Nothing to Say* was going to be the title. But an informal poll of friends revealed two camps: those who hated it, and those who loved it. "Who's going to buy a book by an author who has nothing to say?" they opined. Okay, they had a good point. But their opponents liked the irony (probably because they knew me. I almost *always* have something to say.) Ultimately, I even tried a random survey to see if I could float some ideas out there and make them stick. But nothing really clicked.

Then one day at work I was talking with a friend about the art of finding answers within by listening to one's own intuition. It was one of the true gifts I received from my cancer experience, a gift I hadn't taken out of the box myself for awhile. So I came home that evening with the last draft of the manuscript in hand and decided I would just sit for thirty minutes and meditate. I knew the title was there somewhere; I just had to listen for it.

Sure enough, a title came. It was nothing I had thought of before, and it made perfect sense because it conveyed my *feelings* about my experience, but once I put pen to paper I just couldn't get my head around how it would look on the cover. It just wasn't quite right. So I waited. I sat on my deck watching the sky turn dark over the mountain top, and I waited for the feeling of the title to float through me. That's when it happened. Just as Dorothy's red shoes were her ticket home, the title was there all along, throughout the story and on the back of Laura's postcard in Italian: *non tutto il male viene nuo per nuocere.* Not all bad comes to harm you. It was perfect.

Writing this book as been both a catharsis and a challenge, and I thank my dear friends and blog readers who encouraged me to go ahead and do it. I hope it inspired you in some way to see all that is around you and appreciate the life you have today. It won't last long!

As of now, my continued commitment to bicycling and fitness has continued to keep my too-high cancer-antigen blood-test score relatively stable, and I remain healthy, happy, and hopeful for a cure in the coming years. I am also contemplating an early retirement in order to devote my remaining years to something fulfilling and, with any luck, useful. Perhaps another book—who knows?

Thanks for reading.

About the Author

Jan Mock is a trial attorney, amateur bicycle racer, and cancer survivor who lives in Northern California with her wife, Carole, and their two tiny, red teacup poodles, Madison and Madeleine.

Printed in the United States
By Bookmasters